Chris Wiegand

FEDERICO FELLINI

Ringmaster of Dreams 1920 – 1993

TASCHEN

KÖLN LONDON LOS ANGELES MADRID PARIS TOKYO

FRONT COVER
Still from 'La dolce vita' (1960)
Sylvia (Anita Ekberg) experiences a symbolic
rebirth in the waters of Rome's Trevi Fountain.

FIRST PAGE
Still from '8 1/2' (1963)
The opening dream sequence, where Guido
floats into the air.

FRONTISPIECE
On the set of 'The Clowns' (1970)
Federico Fellini.

THIS PAGE
1 **Federico Fellini** Showing how to play a scene.
2 **Federico Fellini** He enjoyed playing instruments
on the set. 3 **On the set of 'The Voice of the
Moon' (1990)** Fellini has fun with Roberto
Benigni.

OPPOSITE PAGE
On the set of 'Fellini's Satyricon' (1969)

PAGES 6/7
On the set of 'Roma' (1972)
Fellini demonstrates the correct way to stab
Caesar in the back.

BACK COVER
On the set of 'Fellini's Satyricon' (1969)
Federico Fellini in his trademark hat.

© 2003 TASCHEN GmbH
Hohenzollernring 53, D–50672 Köln
www.taschen.com
Editor/Layout: Paul Duncan/Wordsmith Solutions
Typeface Design: Sense/Net, Andy Disl, Cologne

Printed in Italy
ISBN 3–8228–1590–X

Notes
A superscript number indicates a reference to a note on page 191.

Images
British Film Institute Stills, Posters and Designs, London:
1, 4left+centre, 5, 8, 10, 12, 14/15, 16, 17, 18/19, 20, 22 (2),
23 (2), 24/25, 27, 28top, 29t, 32, 34, 39, 40 (2), 41, 44/45, 48,
52 (2), 53 (2), 60, 61, 63, 67, 69, 70, 71, 74, 75, 76, 77, 78,
80 (2), 81 (2), 84 (2), 85t, 86/87, 88 (2), 90, 92/93, 95, 96, 97,
100, 108bottom, 113, 114, 115, 128, 130 (2), 131, 134b, 136b,
137b, 140t, 153 (2), 157, 159t, 160b, 162t, 170, 175t, 181,
Back Cover
PWE Verlag / defd-movies, Hamburg:
Front Cover, 2, 4r, 6/7, 13 (2), 28b, 30, 31 (2), 33, 35, 36/37,
38 (2), 42, 46, 47, 49, 56, 57, 59 (2), 62, 64, 65, 66, 68, 72,
82, 89, 94, 104, 106/107, 108t, 109 (2), 110/111, 134t, 144t,
145b, 150, 152 (2), 154/155, 158, 159b, 160t, 161 (2), 162b,
164, 166, 167 (2), 168/169, 171 (2), 172, 175b, 176, 177,
182/183, 187, 188 (5), 189, 190
Herbert Klemens / Filmbild Fundus Robert Fischer, Munich:
85b, 91, 98/99, 102/103, 116, 117, 118/119, 120, 121, 124,
125, 132, 135 (2), 136t, 137t, 140b, 141, 142, 143 (2), 144b,
145t, 146, 147, 148/149, 173, 178, 179
The Kobal Collection, London/New York: 54/55, 122, 123, 126/127,
138/139, 163
Studio Patellani/Corbis, London: 50, 51
Timepix, New York: 11 (Pix Inc), 129 (Carlo Bavagnoli)
Hulton Getty Archive, London: 192

Copyright
The film images in this book are copyright to the respective
distributors: Capitolium Film (*Luci del varietà*), PDC-OFI (*Lo
sceicco bianco*), Peg Films-Cité Films (*I vitelloni*), Carlo Ponti &
Dino De Laurentiis (*La strada*), Titanus & SGG (*Il bidone*), Dino
De Laurentiis/Les Films Marceau (*Le notti di Cabiria*), Riama
Film/Pathé Consortium Cinema (*La dolce vita*), Concordia
Compagnia Cinematografica and Cineriz/Francinex and Gray
Films (*Le tentazioni del dottor Antonio*), Cineriz/Francinex (*8 1/2*),
Federiz/Francoriz (*Giulietta degli spiriti*), PEA/Les Productions
Artistes Associés (*Fellini-Satyricon*), RAI/ORTF/Bavaria Film/
Compagnia Leone Cinematografica (*I clowns*), Ultra Film/Les
Productions Artistes Associés (*Roma*), FC Produzioni/PECF
(*Amarcord*), PEA (*Il Casanova di Federico Fellini*), Daime
Cinematografica S.p.A. and RAI-TV/Albatros Produktion GmbH
(*Prova d'orchestra*), Opera Film/Gaumont (*La città delle donne*),
RAI/Vides Produzione/Gaumont (*E la nave va*), PEA/REVCOM
Films, Les Films Ariane, FR3 Films Production, Stella Film, Anthea,
RAI-Uno (*Ginger e Fred*), Aljosha Production/RAI-Uno/Cinecittà
(*Intervista*), Mario and Vittorio Cecchi Gori, for C.G. Group
Tiger-Cinemax/RAI (*La voce della luna*). We deeply regret it if,
despite our concerted efforts, any copyright owners have been
unintentionally overlooked and omitted. Obviously we will amend
any such errors in the next edition if they are brought to the
attention of the publisher.

CONTENTS

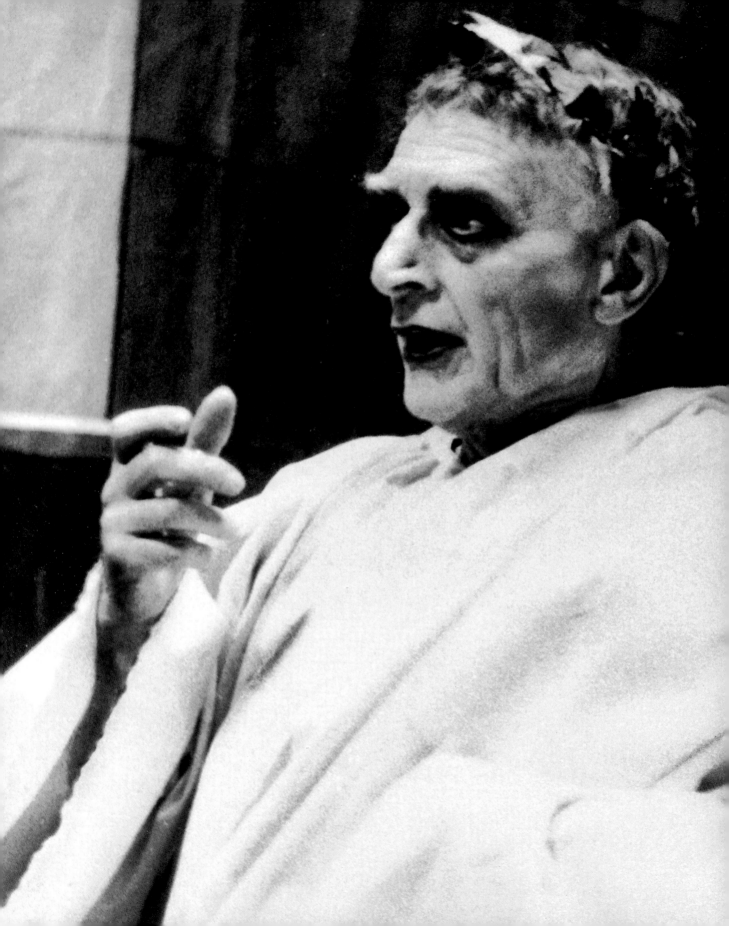

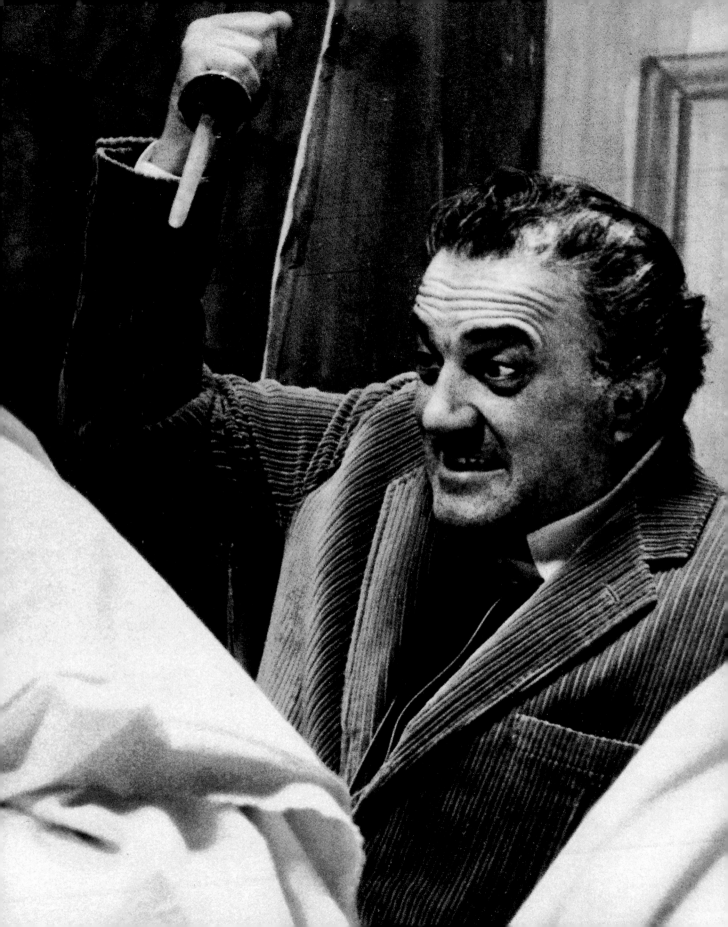

From Rimini to Rome 1920–1950

On 29 March 1993 Federico Fellini was awarded his fifth Oscar, a lifetime achievement statuette to add to a quartet of Best Foreign Language Film awards for *La strada* (*The Road*, 1954), *Le notti di Cabiria* (*The Nights of Cabiria*, 1957), *Otto e mezzo* (*8 1/2*, 1963) and *Amarcord* (*I Remember*, 1973). The 73-year-old director, suffering from acute arthritis, found the journey to California for the ceremony something of a challenge. He arrived at the Dorothy Chandler Pavilion with the support of an entourage that included Giulietta Masina, his wife and muse, and Marcello Mastroianni, the actor long known as his onscreen alter ego. The group found themselves jostled by hordes of photographers, cameramen and journalists. The scene wouldn't have been out of place in *La dolce vita* (1960), the kaleidoscopic masterpiece that propelled Fellini to international fame, earning him the title *il maestro* in his native country.

Fellini was handed the award by Sophia Loren, who described him as "one of the screen's master storytellers" – a fitting title for a director who had also been variously a journalist, caricaturist, gagman and scriptwriter. A showman who referred to himself as a puppeteer, ringmaster and inventor, Fellini was a master storyteller above all else throughout those careers. The many journalists who interviewed him at Cinecittà studios would tell you as much. Like all great storytellers, he was also an expert liar. Prone to self-mythologising and fond of ambiguity, the enigmatic director rejected *cinéma-vérité* in favour of what he called "cine-mendacity." His comments ranged from the elliptical to the infuriating: in his work, "everything and nothing" was autobiographical. If Fellini was *il maestro* then he was also *il mago*: a talented magician who not only told spellbinding tales on the screen, but also span magical yarns about his life story. 'I have invented myself entirely,' he claimed. 'A childhood, a personality, longings, dreams and memories, all in order to enable me to tell them.'[1]

Consequently, Fellini's biographers often find themselves in muddy waters. Stories re-appear from interview to interview, but dates change, characters evaporate and details blur. For Fellini, real-life memories and celluloid fantasies were clearly interchangeable. Reflecting on the director, one is reminded of the Kris Kristofferson lyric quoted in *Taxi Driver* (1976), which was directed by a huge Fellini fan, Martin Scorsese. "He's a walkin' contradiction / partly truth and

On the set of '8 1/2' (1963)
Fellini cracks the whip.

"I believe the film world must be analogous to the world of the circus, where the bond between the bearded lady, the Lilliputians, the trapeze artists, the clowns, is greater than the one they have with their normal brothers and sisters who live 'civilian' lives away from the circus."

Federico Fellini[24]

partly fiction."[2] This book looks at the "walking contradiction" that was Italian cinema's greatest poet.

The son of Urbano, a travelling salesman from Savignano, and Ida, a housewife from Rome, Federico Fellini was born on 20 January 1920 in the small Adriatic resort of Rimini. He was the eldest of three children. A brother, Riccardo, was born in 1921, and a sister, Maddalena, followed in 1929. Fellini had little in common with his siblings and felt estranged from his distant, repressive parents. A sickly child, suffering from a thyroid imbalance that left him self-consciously skinny, he withdrew into his startlingly rich imagination at an early age. He also comforted himself with a range of art forms. His first trip to the circus, aged seven, left a lasting impression. Variety shows at the local theatre had the same effect. Rimini's Fulgor Cinema quickly became a home away from home. Fellini visited the picture house religiously, marvelling at the comic escapades of the Marx Brothers, Laurel and Hardy, Charlie Chaplin and Harold Lloyd.

Fellini soon knew that his calling was in the liberating world he saw onstage and on the screen. By the age of nine he was putting on shows with handmade puppets. A precociously talented artist, he filled sketchbooks with fevered drawings of balloon-breasted women and cartoon heroes, copied painstakingly from the pages of children's magazines. In the most popular of these, *Il corriere dei Piccoli*, Fellini read influential American comic strips like *Bringing Up Father*, *Felix the Cat* and *Happy Hooligan*. He picked up comic techniques from artists such as Frederick Burr Opper, Alexander Raymond and George McManus.

In later life Fellini claimed that such artistic expression provided him with an escape route from his stifling days at boarding school in Fano. Official documentation reveals that it was his brother Riccardo, and not Federico, who attended the school. Fellini also infamously circulated a story that he ran away to join a travelling circus. But as he eventually admitted to Charlotte Chandler, "I would like to have been with the circus for months, but it was more like an afternoon."[3] These claims reveal the kind of romantic childhood Fellini wished for himself.

As he developed his skills as a caricaturist, Fellini began to sign his work with the name 'Fellas.' He sent anonymous work – mostly sketches, cartoons and comic one-liners – to the weekly supplement *La Domenica del corriere*. In 1937 he left school with a diploma in classical studies and opened an art shop with Demos Bonini, an acquaintance. Fellini sketched designs, signing himself 'Fe,' while Demos added the colour, leaving the name 'Bo.' Their collaborative work was reflected in the shop's name: FEBO. As Fellini's reputation grew, he engineered a deal with the manager of the Fulgor. In exchange for free entrance he drew caricatures of contemporary actors, in the manner of Nino Za, a renowned contemporary Italian caricaturist. The drawings hung in the Fulgor's foyer and local shop windows as adverts for the cinema's current programme.

In 1937 Fellini left for Florence, where he stayed for a few months, earning a meagre living drawing cartoons and sketches for the satirical magazine *420*. From Florence, he moved to Rome. Fellini had felt a special connection to the Eternal City since his youth, partly because his mother was born there. Promising his mother he would enrol at the university's law faculty, he arrived in Rome in January 1938. He lived at first in rented rooms scattered throughout the city and became something of a flâneur, walking the streets and soaking up the atmo-

ABOVE
Federico Fellini

OPPOSITE
Riccardo and Federico Fellini (1925)
The brothers play on the beach of their home town, Rimini. The beach is a recurring motif of Federico's movies and is the place where his characters achieve self-realisation.

sphere. He immediately fell in love with the place, and it became the home he rarely left for the next 50 years.

In 1939 he found work as a vignettist for *Marc'Aurelio*, an influential and subversive publication modelled in part on *Punch*. He contributed prolifically to the magazine for three years and also gathered all kinds of other experience. He wrote short stories, advertising copy, gags for the comedian Macario and worked as a journalist interviewing actors and directors. For extra money he drew caricatures for customers in restaurants. Fellini's diverse talents and powers of persuasion opened doors for him wherever he went. He even succeeded in dodging the draft through a mixture of fate, bribery, cunning and quick thinking.

When Rome was liberated by the Americans in 1944, Fellini found it hard to find work. The film industry was effectively shut down and newspapers and magazines fell into the hands of the Americans. With the assistance of a group of friends he opened The Funny Face Shop, a caricature shop on the via Nazionale. The store, which soon became part of a Roman chain, was frequented almost entirely by American GIs, making the arrival in 1945 of famed Italian film-maker Roberto Rossellini all the more surprising. Rossellini, in his late 30s, had directed six short films and four features, earning a reputation for capturing his subjects in a sensitive, observational light. The director visited Fellini because he was interested in casting Aldo Fabrizi, an acquaintance of the artist, in his new film. Rossellini knew he couldn't afford Fabrizi, so he asked Fellini if he could persuade the actor to take the role of a priest who is killed by an SS firing squad. It was a gritty part, unlike the comic material for which the actor had become known, but Fabrizi was persuaded.

The story about the priest was welded together with one about the role of children in the Resistance, becoming *Roma, città aperta* (*Rome, Open City*, 1945). Fellini worked on the film's screenplay, and it was written in a week, with Rossellini and Sergio Amidei. He was primarily responsible for the development of Fabrizi's character and is credited with lightening the tone of the film, adding significant moments of humour.

Still from 'Rome, Open City' (1945)
Pina and Don Pietro (Aldo Fabrizi). The priest's humorous moments were written by Fellini.

The look and feel of the film, and its socially aware story, revealed a new kind of authentic, vernacular Italian cinema. *Rome, Open City* emerged as the recognised benchmark of neorealism or 'open-air' cinema. Unlike several less accomplished neorealist features it was a domestic hit and also achieved international success, particularly in the United States. Fellini, Rossellini and Amidei subsequently collaborated on the screenplay for *Paisà* (*Paisan*, 1946), another feature that was shot in a similar documentary style. The film used non-professional actors to examine the liberation of war-torn Italy from a number of different perspectives. When Rossellini fell ill during the shoot, Fellini directed one of the six sequences.

Following *Paisà*, Rossellini went on location in war-ravaged Berlin for the black market drama *Germania, anna zero* (*Germany, Year Zero*, 1947). Fellini worked on the screenplays for Duilio Coletti's *Il passatore* (*A Buffet for Stefano*, 1947) and Goffredo Alessandrini's *L'ebreo errante* (*The Wandering Jew*, 1947). On Coletti's film he worked alongside seasoned screenwriter Tullio Pinelli. He collaborated with Pinelli and Rossellini on *Il miracolo* (*The Miracle*), the second episode of *L'amore* (*The Ways of Love*, 1948), a two-part feature directed by Rossellini. For the *Il miracolo* script Fellini drew on childhood

ABOVE
Still from 'Rome, Open City' (1945)
The emotive face of Anna Magnani as Pina.

LEFT
Still from 'Rome, Open City' (1945)
Pina fights the Germans because she wants to
see her husband, who has been arrested.
Running after him, she is shot and killed.

PAGES 14/15
Still from 'Rome, Open City' (1945)
After the execution of Don Pietro, the children
continue the Resistance movement.

*"And here is the real lesson I learned from Roberto
[Rossellini]: this humility before the camera and in
a certain sense this extraordinary faith in things
photographed – in men, in faces."*

Federico Fellini[21]

13

Still from 'Paisà' (1946)
The streetwise kid steals shoes from the drunk soldier. In his quest for his shoes, the soldier discovers the deprivation suffered by the Romans. Fellini added humour to Rossellini's morally complex films.

memories of stories he had heard during summer holidays at his grandmother's in Gambettola. The plot concerns a simple young woman (Anna Magnani) who mistakes a vagrant (played by Fellini) for Saint Joseph. Fellini acted as assistant director on the controversial short.

Fellini balanced his work for the neorealist Rossellini with scriptwriting of a more mainstream nature for Lux, a commercial studio. At Lux, he co-wrote *Senza pietà* (*Without Pity*, 1948), a noir-influenced tale of inter-racial romance which marked Masina's proper screen debut (she appears briefly in *Paisà*). At the start of the next decade he co-wrote *Francesco, giullare di Dio* (*The Flowers of St. Francis*, 1950) and *Europa '51* (*The Greatest Love*, 1952) with Rossellini. The latter, a vehicle for Rossellini's new wife Ingrid Bergman, also starred Giulietta Masina. As the decade progressed, however, the two men drifted apart. Rossellini directed a series of pictures starring Bergman and Fellini helmed his own first films.

ABOVE
Still from 'Paisà' (1946)
The neorealist films pioneered by Roberto
Rossellini used non-actors and real locations
to devastating effect.

PAGES 18/19
On the set of 'Paisà' (1946)
Fellini is just to the left of the camera,
wearing sunglasses.

*"To me, neorealism is a way of seeing reality
without prejudice, without conventions coming
between it and myself – facing it without
preconceptions, looking at it in an honest way –
whatever reality is, not just social reality, but
spiritual reality, metaphysical reality, all that
there is within a man."*

Federico Fellini [21]

The *Maestro* Arrives
1950–1953

Fellini's directorial debut came in 1950, with the assistance of *Without Pity*'s Milanese director Alberto Lattuada, for whom he had co-written three scripts in the late 1940s. Fellini and Lattuada formed a production company, with the assistance of both Giulietta Masina and Carla Del Poggio, Lattuada's wife, to fund *Luci del varietà* (*Variety Lights*, 1950), a sympathetic tale about a group of travelling vaudeville performers. Lattuada and Fellini co-wrote and co-directed the comic vehicle, which had starring roles for their wives. The project was a family affair for Lattuada: his father wrote the score, and his sister acted as production manager.

The film opens with a variety show in a small, packed auditorium. Onstage, an ageing man delivers a musical eulogy for his lost goose and a chorus of bikini-clad beauties dance to a jazzy score. Backstage, an irate gentleman swindled by the troupe in the past confiscates the night's takings. The vaudevillians take a train to the next town, during which disheartened stage veteran Checco (Peppino de Felippo) is accosted by Liliana (Del Poggio), an ambitious ingénue and former beauty queen, who is determined to join the troupe. While Checco is quickly persuaded by her charms, the rest of the revue are unconvinced. Nevertheless, she is incorporated into the act and during that night's performance Liliana's skirt slips off. As a result of the rapturous applause she becomes the new star of the show and swells in self-importance.

Checco loses the support of the troupe and searches for new collaborators to appear with Liliana. He meets a trumpet player and a sharpshooter ("the black man and Buffalo Bill") who he believes can form a new act, but Liliana leaves for another company. Checco returns to his old revue. In the closing scene at the railway station, he meets Liliana one last time as they board separate trains. In the kind of cyclical twist that recurs in Fellini's later films, Checco tries to sign up another potential soubrette as the train pulls out of the station.

An exuberant, eccentric and frequently farcical comedy, *Variety Lights* portrays the world of show business in a manner reminiscent of Hollywood backstage musicals. In his youth, Fellini watched various vaudeville performances and variety acts in Rimini. He declared that he had based the script on firsthand observations from touring with Aldo Fabrizi's revue show. While such claims

On the set of 'Variety Lights' (1950)
Fellini (arms folded to the left of the spotlight) once said that he didn't co-direct the film but that he simply folded his arms and watched Alberto Lattuada do all the work.

"I didn't choose to become a film-maker: it was the cinema that chose me."

Federico Fellini [21]

ABOVE
Still from 'Variety Lights' (1950)
The performers give the impression that
everything is wonderful.

RIGHT
On the set of 'Variety Lights' (1950)
Fellini (right) watches a rehearsal with
Alberto Lattuada (crouched).

ABOVE
Still from 'Variety Lights' (1950)
Liliana Antonelli (Carlo Del Poggio) will do anything in her quest for fame, including wearing less clothes to get more applause from the audience.

LEFT
Still from 'Variety Lights' (1950)
The real lives of the performers take place on the railroads of Italy. They stick together despite the ups and downs caused by their meagre existence. Here Checco Dalmonte (Peppino De Filippo, centre) talks to girlfriend Melina Amour (Giulietta Masina).

PAGES 24/25
Still from 'Variety Lights' (1950)
Edison Will (Giulio Cali) and his goose are abandoned on the tracks.

are false, his general familiarity with the kind of performers in Checco's troupe perhaps accounts for the film's affectionate tone. He told Charlotte Chandler, "I feel a bond with everyone who has the aspiration to make a show."[4] For Fellini, like the old man in his 1985 movie *Ginger e Fred* (*Ginger and Fred*), artists were "the benefactors of humanity."

It is difficult to define the exact contribution of each of the film's directors to this collaborative project. Fellini is quoted at different times as saying, "I wrote the original story, wrote the screenplay, and chose the actors"[5] and "To tell the truth, Lattuada did everything. I just looked on."[6] However the work was divided, the film reveals several key Fellinian concerns, including its bittersweet tone, marginal itinerant characters and musical interludes. Like many protagonists in his later films, the provincial characters in *Variety Lights* are resilient in the face of despair and are, like their creator, in awe of high society. *La strada*, another road story with a similar structure, and *Ginger and Fred* also tell of small-time performers down on their luck. Zampanò in the former, and the ageing hoofers in the latter, are variations on the members of Checco's troupe. Zampanò's act of breaking chains is as pointless and uninspired as that of the fakir who munches broken light bulbs onstage. *Ginger and Fred*, a melancholy swansong to the great variety shows, echoes a poignant closing comment in *Variety Lights*. One of the members of the revue comments that they no longer perform in Trani because only films are now shown at the theatre there.

Variety Lights was neither a critical nor a commercial success, which was a blow for Fellini and Lattuada because they had gone over budget on the production. Its poor performance was partly caused by the concurrent release of the more successful *Vita da cani* (*A Dog's Life*), a film set in a similar milieu. Fellini continued to work on screenplays for other directors and co-wrote three films for Pietro Germi including *La città si difende* (*The City Defends Itself*, 1951). He also co-wrote *Persiane chiuse* (*Drawn Shutters*, 1951) with Tullio Pinelli and was called upon to act as stand-in director on the film. Its producer, Luigi Rovere, was so impressed by his work that he invited Fellini to direct and co-write *Lo sceicco bianco* (*The White Sheik*, 1952), a satire on the contemporary popularity of *fumetti*. A kind of adult comic strip using photographs in place of cartoons, *fumetti* told romantic adventures for a mature, mostly female, readership. The initial treatment for the film was written by Michelangelo Antonioni, who had just completed a documentary about *fumetti*, entitled *L'amorosa menzogna* (1949).

Still from 'Variety Lights' (1950)
Melina is the moral centre of the film, remaining true to herself and others. This is the type of role often taken by Giulietta Masina.

ABOVE
Still from 'The White Sheik' (1952)
On a visit to Rome, Wanda Cavalli spends the day away from her husband to pursue the White Sheik (Alberto Sordi), who appears dashing and charming.

RIGHT
Still from 'The White Sheik' (1952)
Ivan Cavalli (Leopoldo Trieste) timetabled every moment of the trip to Rome. When his wife disappears his life becomes chaotic.

ABOVE
Still from 'The White Sheik' (1952)
Wanda Cavalli (Brunella Bovo) dreams of the
romantic White Sheik, the star of her favourite
fumetti (photo-novels). "Dreams are our true
life," she says.

ABOVE
Still from 'The White Sheik' (1952)
He is as romantic as she had dreamed.

LEFT
Still from 'The White Sheik' (1952)
Wanda is so mesmerised by the White Sheik that she dresses up for the *fumetti* photo shoot, becoming Fatma, the White Sheik's faithful slave.

OPPOSITE
Still from 'The White Sheik' (1952)
When Wanda first sees the White Sheik he is swinging on a high trapeze.

Still from 'The White Sheik' (1952)
To revenge himself on his absent wife, Ivan spends the night in the company of two prostitutes, Cabiria and Silvana.

The White Sheik uses a classical, three-act structure rarely seen in Fellini's later work. It follows a pair of provincial newlyweds, Wanda (Brunella Bovo) and Ivan (Leopoldo Trieste), honeymooning in Rome. Wanda is quiet and impressionable; Ivan officious and irritable. Each arrives in Rome with a separate agenda. Ivan seizes the opportunity to explore the city, drawing up a packed schedule for their stay. Wanda takes the chance to track down Fernando Rivoli (Alberto Sordi), the handsome star of *The White Sheik,* her favourite photostrip. Shortly after their arrival Wanda gives Ivan the slip and heads for the photostrip's editorial office. She discovers that Rivoli is posing for a new photo shoot and heads off to meet him in Fregene, leaving her luckless husband to explain her absence to his relatives. Wanda is thrilled to star as a harem girl in the shoot but the Sheik's intentions are less than honourable. She leaves distraught and attempts to drown herself in the Tiber. Her suicide bid is unsuccessful and she returns to Ivan, who refuses to hear her excuses. The honeymoon continues, with Wanda realising that it is Ivan who is her real White Sheik.

In his first full feature, Fellini displays a level of directorial flair unseen in *Variety Lights.* Succinctly flitting between Wanda and Ivan's separate adventures over a 24-hour period, he employs a complex system of cross-cutting. This parallel editing gives the film a considerable screwball pace, aided by Nino Rota's typically exuberant musical refrains. *The White Sheik* shares many similarities

with *Variety Lights*. Both rely on observational, character-based situation comedy. The tawdry group of models and oddballs, packed off from the photostrip's offices for each amateurish shoot, recalls Checco's ragged variety company. The troubled balance between fantasy and reality, illusion and self-delusion, as seen in the earlier film, also returns here. When reading the *fumetti* Wanda indulges in escapist fantasies. "Our real life is in our dreams," she muses.

As a satire on the world of *fumetti*, the film lacks the kind of bite that the plot at first suggests and that the material really demands. Fellini tries to be both sympathetic and satirical, his identification with provincial dreamers like Wanda softening the film's impact. Critics were subsequently puzzled by its confused tone. Was it supposed to be a baroque romance or a social satire? It was poorly received at the Venice Film Festival and fared little better when released. Some laid the blame on the casting of Trieste, who was better known as a scriptwriter, and Sordi, who had little popularity as an actor. A talented comic, Sordi had previously appeared in *Il delitto di Giovanni Episcopo* (*The Crime of Giovanni Episcopo*, 1947), which Fellini had co-written while at Lux.

Still from 'The White Sheik' (1952)
In reality, the White Sheik is unemployed butcher Fernando Rivoli, who uses his position to pursue his desires, much like Checco Dalmonte in 'Variety Lights'.

Still from 'I vitelloni' (1953)
The layabouts fritter away their time gambling at pool tables.

"…*Rimini features not only in* I vitelloni, La strada, Amarcord *and* Roma, *but even in those films which have no points of reference to my native town, like* La dolce vita, Satyricon, Casanova, And the Ship Sails On, *where the action always takes place against the distant backdrop of the sea – like a primordial element, a blue line cutting across the sky – whence arrive the pirate ships, the Turks, the King, the American battle cruisers with Ginger Rogers and Fred Astaire dancing in the shadow of the guns."*

Federico Fellini [20]

Despite its poor initial reception, *The White Sheik* is today considered a classic Italian comedy. Its undeniable charm is characteristic of Fellini's first films. One scene in particular pre-empts the world of his next feature. In conversation with the woman at the editorial office, Wanda talks about her small provincial hometown, which she says is filled with "vulgar people… young men with no conversation." *I vitelloni* (*Spivs, The Young and the Passionate*, 1953) follows one such group of men. Another gentle satire, co-written by Fellini, Pinelli and Ennio Flaiano, the film follows a group of *vitelloni*, or layabouts. (The word is taken from the slang expression *vaudellone*, which means 'fat gut.') Supported by their parents, they live an opaque existence in a small coastal town. Imagine François Truffaut's mischievous *mistons* a few more years down the line.

The five *vitelloni* are first seen marching through the streets in the title sequence. The intellectual Leopoldo (Leopoldo Trieste) is an amateur playwright. Effeminate Alberto (Alberto Sordi) lives with his sister, who is involved with a married man. Riccardo (Riccardo Fellini) is a talented tenor. Moraldo (Franco Interlenghi), the youngest of the group, is an amiable dreamer. His sister, Sandra (Eleonora Ruffo), is romantically involved with outrageous womaniser Fausto (Franco Fabrizi), the group's leader and ill-chosen 'spiritual guide.'

At the start of the film Sandra discovers she is pregnant. Fausto, the father to be, immediately tries to skip town. His father catches him and forces him to

ABOVE
Still from 'I vitelloni' (1953)
Moraldo (Franco Interlenghi, right) and friends
sample the café culture.

PAGES 36/37
Still from 'I vitelloni' (1953)
The young men are trapped in a claustrophobic
world of family and relationships, which leads to
their inevitable spiritual stagnation.

marry Sandra. While they honeymoon in Rome, the other *vitelloni* roam around
the town, shooting pool and chasing women. On the couple's return, Fausto's
father-in-law gets him a job as an errand boy at a local shop. He soon returns
to his womanising ways and is fired for making a move on the boss's wife.
News of his behaviour reaches Sandra but Moraldo saves his friend's reputation
by lying. Shortly after, Sandra gives birth. Fausto slips up again and this time
Moraldo can't excuse his behaviour. Sandra leaves, taking the baby with her.
Fausto eventually finds her and declares himself a changed man. In the closing
scene, Moraldo leaves town in search of a better life in the middle of the night.
One of the *vitelloni* finally leaves the nest.

The *vitelloni*, like the vaudevillians in *Variety Lights* and the young Fellini in
Rimini, all dream of escaping the provinces for the big city. In light of his departure at the end of the picture, Moraldo seems a surrogate for Fellini, who narrates the picture himself. Nevertheless, the director was quick to point out that
he was never a *vitellone* himself: "I knew those idle heroes of the seaside cafes
from a distance and invented every single thing about them."[7] Like Rimini,
the unnamed backwater of the film is a resort town. The sea forms a symbolic
landscape in many of the director's films, especially *La strada* and *E la nave va*
(*And the Ship Sails On*, 1983). The deserted piazza, as seen in the striking opening and the post-carnival scene, is also a recurrent image. Public gatherings

ABOVE
Still from 'I vitelloni' (1953)
Fellini used public events to define the characters and their relationships. The film begins with the 'Miss Mermaid' beauty pageant and the revelation that the winner, Sandra, is pregnant.

RIGHT
Still from 'I vitelloni' (1953)
Sandra (Eleonora Ruffo) marries Fausto (Franco Fabrizi), the father of her child, surrounded by the 'vitelloni': Riccardo (Riccardo Fellini), Moraldo and Leopoldo (Leopoldo Trieste).

(*I vitelloni* has a beauty contest, a wedding and a carnival) recur in the director's
work, often in the shape of outlandish parties. Later films also open or close with
scenes set at railways.

I vitelloni reveals Fellini's increasingly sophisticated and mature directorial
style. When Sandra faints at the beauty contest he makes effective use of a crop
of close-ups. For the ending he uses a series of dramatic pans, showing four of
the *vitelloni* at home, seemingly observed from the departing train that takes
the fifth away for good. This subjective style is adopted in later films. Fellini's
particular achievement here is his masterly control of tone. He creates a tale
that is in turn comic, poignant and even tragic. He also does well handling the
film's large cast. For the first time, Fellini uses rounded characters as opposed
to caricatures, although some, including Riccardo (played by his brother), are
thinly drawn.

I vitelloni won Fellini unexpected international attention and, for the first
time as a director, a distribution deal. It also won him his first award – one of
six Silver Lions that were handed out at Venice that year. So successful was the
film, Fellini considered directing a sequel to it. In 1954 he wrote a script entitled
Moraldo in città (Moraldo in the City), charting the character's continued adven-

ABOVE
Still from 'I vitelloni' (1953)
Although Fausto is newly married to Sandra,
he still has his eye on other women (Arlette
Sauvage, left). He is the model for future Fellini
womanisers.

RIGHT
On the set of 'I vitelloni' (1953)
Fellini (right) discusses the script with
Jean Brochard (left).

tures. The sequel never materialised but parts of the script ended up in later films. The dilemma of Fellini's *vitelloni* has been replayed by the frequenters of Barry Levinson's *Diner* (1982), the teenagers driving around a Californian "turkey town" in George Lucas's *American Graffiti* (1973) and the small time hoods striking deals in New York's Little Italy in Martin Scorsese's *Mean Streets* (1973). Gabriele Muccino's recent domestic hit *L'ultimo bacio* (*The Last Kiss*, 2001) shows a similar group of characters struggling to come to terms with romantic commitment and other responsibilities, clinging hopelessly to their adolescence.

Upon completion of *I vitelloni*, Fellini directed a short episode for a compilation film, *Amore in città* (*Love in the City*, 1953), conceived by the diehard neorealist Cesare Zavattini. Zavattini stressed the importance of reality in cinema, declaring, "It should accept, unconditionally, what is contemporary."[8] He envisioned *Love in the City* as a kind of celluloid newspaper and commissioned six investigations into daily life in contemporary Italy, shot in the neorealist fashion using only non-professional actors. The other contributors included Lattuada, Antonioni, Francesco Maselli, Dino Risi and Carlo Lizzani.

Fellini's short, *Un'agenzia matrimoniale* (*A Matrimonial Agency*, 1953), told a humorous tale in the same vein as *The White Sheik*. Despite Zavattini's demand that the stories presented be realistic, Fellini dreamt up a story about a journalist who goes undercover at a marriage agency, where he pretends to represent a werewolf friend of his who is looking for love. (His joke backfires when a sensitive young woman declares an interest in meeting the werewolf.) Fellini followed Zavattini's instructions more closely when it came to casting, using drama students from Cinecittà's neighbouring Centro Sperimentale. A work of limited importance to those studying the Fellini canon, this 20-minute short is nevertheless the highlight of an uninspired collection. It marks the first of Fellini's contributions to episodic films – he shot two more in the 1960s. The solitary nature of the film's protagonist prefigures the loners of *Il bidone* (*The Swindle, The Swindlers*, 1955), *The Nights of Cabiria* and the journalist played by Marcello Mastroianni in *La dolce vita*. Its ludicrously fictitious plot revealed Fellini's rejection of neorealism. The director was now ready to turn away from the movement that was so influential to his first features, in pursuit of his own poetic, personal style of film-making.

Still from 'I vitelloni' (1953)
Moraldo is a dreamer. He does not get involved with domestic arrangements or provincial life and eventually decides to leave the seaside town, as Fellini did.

Three Films of Redemption 1954–1957

A trio of films directed in the mid-1950s saw Fellini transcend his neorealist origins. *La strada*, *Il bidone* and *The Nights of Cabiria*, often grouped together as the 'films of redemption,' display the director's move from neorealism to a kind of fantastical individualism. Heavily symbolic tales of innocence betrayed, they feature marginal characters searching in unusual places for spiritual salvation.

Fellini originally envisioned *La strada* as the follow-up to *The White Sheik* but disagreed with his original producer over the casting for the film. A lyrical fable co-written with Pinelli, it follows the fortunes of Gelsomina (Masina), a simple peasant girl sold by her family to Zampanò (Anthony Quinn), a cruel and brutish circus performer. Gelsomina is swiftly incorporated into Zampanò's strongman act (he breaks chains by expanding his lungs), and the pair travel together around provincial Italy. On the road, Gelsomina learns the art of comedy, becoming a competent clown. She strives to form an emotional bond with Zampanò but he is incapable of this. Frustrated and homesick, she attempts to leave, but he captures her and beats her. His violent habits are further exposed when the couple join a circus – he is imprisoned for assaulting the Fool (Richard Basehart), the troupe's resident tightrope walker. When released from prison he attacks him again, and the Fool dies in front of Gelsomina's eyes. Devastated by the incident, she withdraws inside herself, fearful of the strongman's powers. Zampanò deserts her. Five years later news of her death reaches him. Suddenly realising how he felt for her, and overcome with loneliness and regret, Zampanò breaks down by the sea.

The magical and at times over-sentimental *La strada* was shot in Viterbo, Begnoregio and Ovindoli. As suggested by its title, it is both a road movie and a picaresque tale in the vein of Antonioni's *Il grido* (*The Cry*, 1957). The film foreshadows another spiritual journey in *La dolce vita*. Fellini favoured the picaresque structure, allowing his itinerant heroes to observe alternative ways of life and different value systems through influential encounters. His later films share *La strada*'s rhythm – its alternation of lively scenes with quiet ones, daytime episodes with night-time ones. Eschewing the class criticism for which neorealism had become known, *La strada* is a universal human drama that strives to realise what Fellini described as the "joint experience between man and man."

OPPOSITE
Still from 'The Nights of Cabiria' (1957)
The Roman prostitute Cabiria (Giulietta Masina) at a moment of transformation.

PAGES 44/45
Still from 'La strada' (1954)
Zampanò (Anthony Quinn) is a brutish strongman who enjoys flaunting his power.

"All my films turn upon this idea. There is an effort to show a world without love, characters full of selfishness, people exploiting one another, and, in the midst of it all, there is always - and especially in the films with Giulietta - a little creature who wants to give love and who lives for love."

Federico Fellini[21]

A resonant fairy tale about loneliness, it is reminiscent of *Beauty and the Beast*. It also reveals traditional Christian values, most notably in the relationship between Zampanò and the good-willed Gelsomina, who teaches him how to give in to emotional reasoning.

Fellini described *La strada* as a catalogue of his mythical world. It is rich in potent and often ironic imagery. To earn a living, Zampanò breaks free from iron chains, yet keeps his assistant a virtual slave. Catholic symbolism reverberates through the film, with the angelic Gelsomina frequently cast as a religious figure. In one scene she is framed against a poster announcing 'Immaculate Madonna.' The Fool is presented as a Christ-like figure and is shown teaching a parable to Gelsomina. Basehart's innocent countenance adds to the analogy – in *Il bidone* his character, Picasso, says, "I look like an angel." Critics have long debated the importance of the 'trinity' of central characters. The American critic Pauline Kael thought the Fool represented the 'mind,' the strongman the 'body' and Gelsomina the 'soul.'

Fellini argued with his producers over who should play the main roles in the film. Burt Lancaster, who had once been a circus performer, was considered for the role of Zampanò, a character inspired by Fellini's memories of a fearsome pig castrator in Gambettola, one of the towns of his childhood. Quinn, famous for his appearances in Elia Kazan's *Viva Zapata!* (1952) and Vincente Minnelli's *Lust for Life* (1956), won the role instead. He later became typecast as a similarly monosyllabic, meta-masculine figure but none of his subsequent appearances captured the feral, seemingly impenetrable quality he portrayed as Zampanò. Even though his performance in *La strada* was praised, it was Masina's that received the most column space.

Masina had previously starred alongside both Quinn and Basehart in *Donne proibite* (*Angels of Darkness*, 1953). The producers were unconvinced by Fellini's choice, believing the 33-year-old actress to be too old. In the film, however, Gelsomina is as ageless as she is sexless. With her bowler hat, scruffy clothes and distinctive physical performance, Masina's wide-eyed and round-faced peasant girl brought comparisons with Jacques Tati and Charlie Chaplin. Chaplin's tramp and Fellini's Gelsomina share similar gestures. Both are reminiscent of the anarchical Auguste clown – the white clown's dirty brother in the European circus tradition. Gelsomina also recalls the titular hero of the *Happy Hooligan* comic strip. Like so many Fellinian creations, she was born in his sketchbook.

Gelsomina remained the favourite of all the director's characters. So potent was Masina's performance, the public cried out for a sequel. Manufacturers of dolls and sweets chased the rights to the character and there was even talk of an animated cartoon. Fellini would have none of it. The film was a resounding success. It performed well at the Italian box office and Rota's score proved exceptionally popular. Fellini was once more awarded Venice's Silver Lion and received the first-ever Oscar for Best Foreign Language Film. The film, which was later turned into a ballet in Milan, amassed over 50 additional awards.

ABOVE
Still from 'La strada' (1954)
Although Gelsomina (Giulietta Masina) is brutalised by life on the road, her inner strength allows her a kind of serenity.

OPPOSITE
Still from 'La strada' (1954)
Gelsomina is the impish, gentle clown.

"Giulietta [Masina] has the lightness of a phantom, a dream, an idea. She possesses the movements, the mimic skills and the cadences of a clown."

Federico Fellini [20]

Still from 'La strada' (1954)
Zampanò breaks chains for a living but he
keeps Gelsomina chained to him.

Still from 'La strada' (1954)
Afraid to voice her displeasure, Gelsomina's
only recourse is to make faces.

On the set of 'La strada' (1954)
Giulietta Masina remains in character as
Federico Fellini makes adjustments to her
posture and dress.

On the set of 'La strada' (1954)
Make-up is applied to Giulietta Masina.

ABOVE
Still from 'La strada' (1954)
Life on the road means performing in all
conditions, whether it is at a circus…

RIGHT
Still from 'La strada' (1954)
…or at a country wedding.

ABOVE
Still from 'La strada' (1954)
The Fool (Richard Basehart) is a tightrope walker who has his head in the clouds.

LEFT
Still from 'La strada' (1954)
However, the Fool is also a poet and dreamer. He shows Gelsomina how beautiful life could be if she broke free of Zampanò.

PAGES 54/55
On the set of 'La strada' (1954)
Richard Basehart is the first in a long line of international actors to grace Fellini's films.

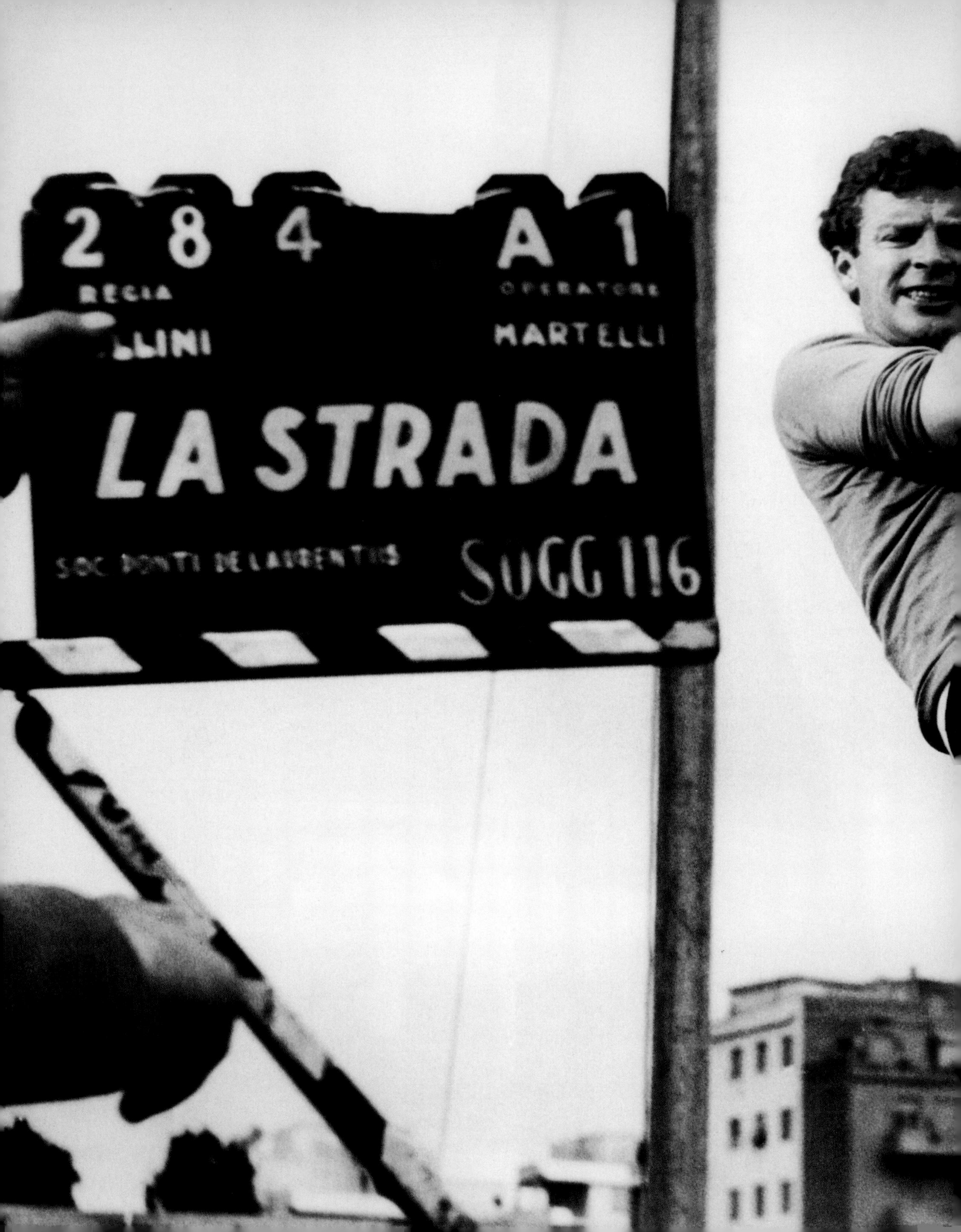
2 8 4
A 1
REGIA
OPERATORE
MARTELLI
LA STRADA
SOGG 116

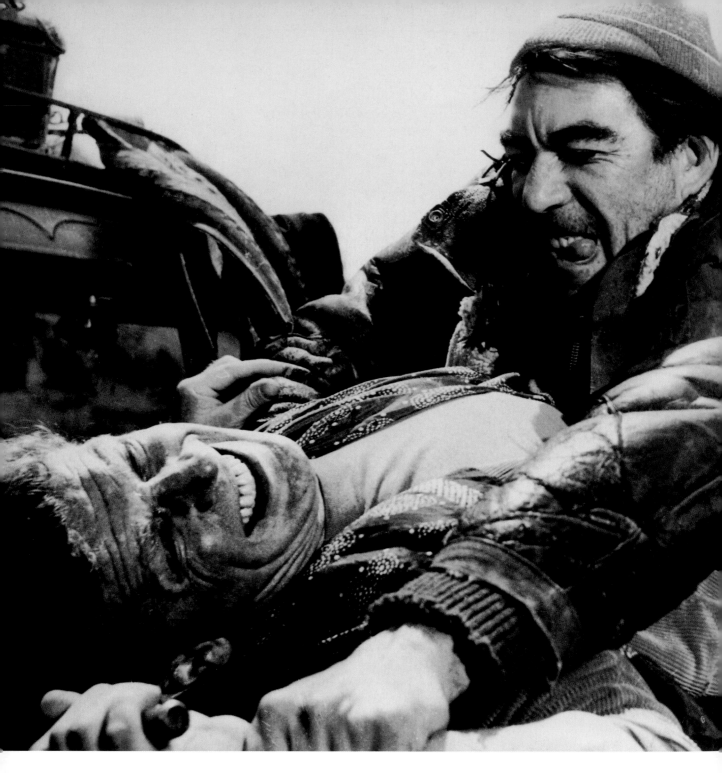

Still from 'La strada' (1954)
Enraged by the Fool's taunts, Zampanò attacks
and accidentally kills him.

Still from 'La strada' (1954)
Gelsomina never recovers from the Fool's death and wanders the countryside alone. It is only when Zampanò hears of her death years later that he becomes human and feels pain for the first time.

Such accolades for *La strada* didn't make the hunt for funding for Fellini's next project, *Il bidone*, any easier. After *La strada*, the producers all wanted Gelsomina. Fellini rejected the lucrative option of returning to these established characters. For his next film he once more chose characters from the lower rungs of the social ladder. *Il bidone*, shot between May and July 1955, follows a bunch of small time crooks akin to the shifty con man in *La strada*.

The action in *Il bidone* unfolds over five days. Once more there are three central characters. Augusto (Broderick Crawford), Picasso (Basehart) and Roberto (Franco Fabrizi) are tricksters who use a variety of shameless scams to hoodwink simple villagers out of their cash. One scheme sees them dressing as priests and charging their victims for saying mass for the souls of the dead. In another they take deposits for new apartments from impoverished slum dwellers. The trio live a tightrope existence not dissimilar to that of Basehart's Fool in *La strada*. Sure enough, one day one of them falls. Augusto is recognised by a man who bought fake antibiotics from him six months earlier. The *bidonista* ends up in jail. On his release, he is not a changed man, but he returns to his swindling schemes with new partners in crime. When he tries to cheat his co-workers they attack him and he falls into a ravine. Augusto is left in solitude and realises that after a lifetime of deceiving others the one person he has constantly deceived is himself.

If Fellini's *bidonisti* remind us of his *vitelloni* it is not just because of the re-appearance of Fabrizi. The three confidence men are essentially overgrown kids evading responsibility and reality. Like the *vitelloni*, they chase women and prowl in a drunken pack around empty piazzas, with Fabrizi as the biggest womaniser in both films.

Their pack mentality is highlighted by the apparent need for a leader. While the *vitelloni* saw Fausto as their 'spiritual leader,' Augusto is the 'spiritual grandfather' of the *bidonisti*. The swindlers also harbour romantic aspirations. Picasso's desire to make a name for himself as a painter and Roberto's hopes of becoming a singer recall Leopoldo's dream to make it as a playwright. (Fellini's characters continually aspire to better themselves, from Ivan, who wants to be town clerk, to Marcello Rubini, who wishes he were a respected novelist.)

Known primarily for his appearances in American gangster movies, Broderick Crawford came to Fellini's attention when the latter saw his face on a poster for *All the King's Men* (1949). As ever, it was the actor's visage that won him the part. Faces, Fellini believed, were the human landscape of his pictures. Crawford had a well-deserved reputation as a drunk and, while he fell off the wagon during filming, his expressive performance as the washed-up, small-time criminal is undoubtedly the highlight of the film.

Typically, Fellini presents Augusto as both abuser and victim. He encourages the viewer's sympathy in a handful of key scenes in which the camera pans away from Augusto, emphasising his solitude in certain situations. Alongside Crawford and Fabrizi, Fellini recast Basehart, who had remained in Rome after his appearance in *La strada*. Masina also appears in the film, cast against type as Iris, Picasso's wife – one of a trio of innocent characters used to offset the three crooks. (The others are Augusto's daughter and the crippled girl he meets in the final reel.)

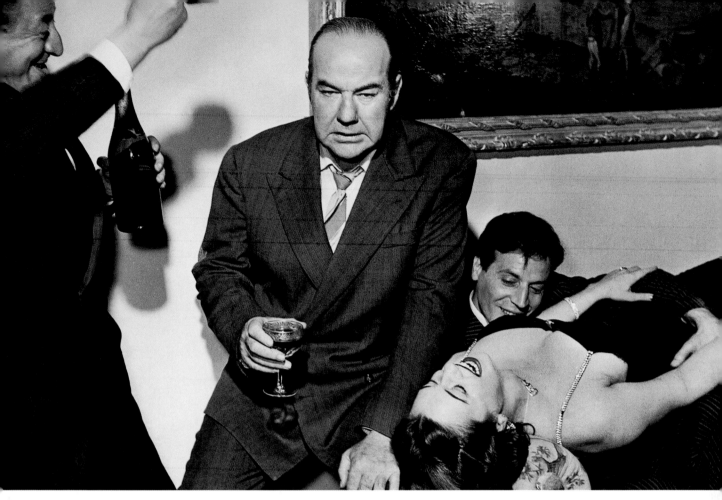

ABOVE
Still from 'Il bidone' (1955)
Augusto (Broderick Crawford) offers his services
to a successful conman but is turned down.
He separated from his wife and daughter to
concentrate on his work and it looks like he'll
never get into the big time.

LEFT
Still from 'Il bidone' (1955)
Iris (Giulietta Masina) finds out that her husband
Picasso (Richard Basehart) earns his money by
conning the poor out of their meagre savings.

Still from 'Il bidone' (1955)
Augusto accidentally meets his estranged daughter Patrizia (Lorella De Luca) and promises her the money she needs to study at university.

Fellini was forced to make extensive cuts to *Il bidone* for its premiere at Venice. He worked against the clock with two editing teams to shape the film as best as possible, but if Fellini had been the hero of the festival in 1954, he proved the villain the following year. *Il bidone* was poorly received, over-shadowed by Antonioni's *Le amiche* (1955) and Dreyer's *Ordet* (*The Word*, 1954). Many found the new film too reminiscent of his earlier works and lacking in their emotional resonance. Further cuts were made before it was released. The final version was structurally flawed and, despite a reduced running time, suffered from a repetitive nature and frequent longueurs. The film bombed in Italy and wasn't released in America until the 1960s. More bitter than sweet, it was Fellini's starkest film yet.

Still from 'Il bidone' (1955)
When the disabled girl Susanna (Sue Ellen Blake) shows complete faith in the Monsignor that Augusto pretends to be, we believe that Augusto may feel remorse for his actions.

Still from 'Il bidone' (1955)
Augusto and Picasso pretend to be priests as
part of a con. The five swindles he performs
show Augusto becoming progressively unhinged
as he experiences a crisis of conscience.

Still from 'Il bidone' (1955)
Augusto is left for dead after double-crossing his colleagues. He dies only moments away from a religious procession saying "…I'm coming with you," which implies his final redemption.

ABOVE
Still from 'The Nights of Cabiria' (1957)
Cabiria is a streetwalker whose vitality, rather than her sexuality, is attractive to men.

OPPOSITE
Still from 'The Nights of Cabiria' (1957)
After being robbed and thrown in the sea by her lover, Cabiria rails against the world.

PAGE 66
Still from 'The Nights of Cabiria' (1957)
Under the influence of the hypnotist (Aldo Silvani, right), Cabiria reveals her trusting and romantic nature.

PAGE 67
Still from 'The Nights of Cabiria' (1957)
Cabiria has a simple and undying faith in the universe, which extends to her religious beliefs.

Il bidone's failure didn't help Fellini find a producer for *The Nights of Cabiria*, another film written for Masina. (The character of Cabiria, a resilient Roman prostitute, originally appeared as a confidante for Ivan in *The White Sheik*, but the role amounted to little more than a cameo.) Numerous producers baulked at Fellini's idea of a film centred on the life of a prostitute. Eventually, Dino de Laurentiis offered Fellini a five-picture contract that would enable him to film the story. When funding became available Fellini threw himself into the project, researching the subject matter by driving around Roman suburbs used by prostitutes as pick-up points. Pier Paolo Pasolini, a young author who had achieved notoriety with his first novel *Ragazzi di vita*, accompanied him. A poet of Roman low life, Pasolini contributed to the film's screenplay, paying particular attention to the dialect spoken by the prostitutes.

The film opens with Cabiria dancing gaily towards the sea with her lover Giorgio who, as she stops to savour the moment, pushes her into the water and disappears with her handbag. Rescued by a group of boys, Cabiria is furious and returns to her little shack on the road to Ostia. She makes a resolution: no more whirlwind romances. When night-time comes, she takes her usual place in the pick-up district of the Passeggiata Archeologica. After an argument with an old prostitute she leaves for via Veneto, where she has a chance encounter with actor Alberto Lazarri (former matinée idol Amedeo Nazzari). Having fallen out with his girlfriend, Lazarri invites Cabiria back to his house for dinner. Cabiria is impressed until his girlfriend returns to make up. She is forced into the closet to hide, reduced to watching Lazarri from a distance, as she has on the screen.

Returning to her friends, Cabiria goes to a religious procession and then visits a variety show, where she is invited onstage by a hypnotist (Aldo Silvani, the circus owner in *La strada*) and put under his spell. In a trance-like state she confides to the audience about her trusting nature. After the show she runs into Oscar (François Périer), a stranger who saw the show. Cabiria slowly falls for his charms and when he proposes, they leave Rome. However, Oscar robs her just like Giorgio before him. The film comes full circle and Cabiria is filled with sorrow. But an encounter with a group of youngsters in a musical procession brings a smile back to her face. Her spirit remains inextinguishable.

For Fellini, Cabiria was Gelsomina's fallen sister. Both are Chaplinesque Auguste figures and the kind of stock types familiar to Italian audiences from the *commedia dell'arte*. Despite her profession, Cabiria remains as asexual as Gelsomina, and both are victims who move between emotional extremes. Cabiria is melancholic and mistreated, but also energetic and indefatigable. Moreover, she is self-sufficient and refuses to work for a pimp. This independence separates the two characters. While Cabiria doesn't think twice about burning her ex-lover's belongings, Gelsomina can only talk of setting fire to Zampanò's possessions. Cabiria's resilience and hopefulness reflected Masina's own character.

The Nights of Cabiria echoes *La strada* through its essentially Christian themes. On her way home from Lazarri's house, Cabiria meets a mysterious gentleman who distributes food to the homeless. This character, 'the man with the sack,' plays the part of a confessor for Cabiria and recognises her solitude. At the time of the film's release, this seven-minute sequence – inspired by a real-

ABOVE
Still from 'The Nights of Cabiria' (1957)
Oscar D'Onofrio (François Périer) asks Cabiria
to marry him and she professes undying love
for him. Having sold her shack to go away with
Oscar, Cabiria is then robbed by him.

OPPOSITE
On the set of 'The Nights of Cabiria' (1957)
Giulietta embraces Fellini after the emotional
cliff-top scene.

PAGE 70
Still from 'The Nights of Cabiria' (1957)
Cabiria's shabby surroundings…

PAGE 71
Still from 'The Nights of Cabiria' (1957)
…are in contrast to her generosity of spirit.

life philanthropist Fellini and designer Piero Gherardi had met in Rome – was
cut. There was uproar about the depiction of an apparently unreligious man
performing religious acts. The problem was emphasised by its juxtaposition
with a scene in which Cabiria attends a religious festival – an experience that
is, in comparison, frightening and overwhelming.

As Cabiria, Masina is required to carry the film single-handed, appearing
in almost every scene. Her astonishing performance won her the Best Actress
award at Cannes in 1956. The film's reputation spread quickly in the United
States, especially when it won an Oscar for Best Foreign Film. When it was
released, *La strada* was still enjoying what would become a three-year run
in New York City, so the two films ran concurrently. *The Nights of Cabiria*
was turned into a popular 1965 Broadway musical, *Sweet Charity*, which
was subsequently adapted for the big screen in 1968.

Superstar Director
1958–1963

Fellini's films of redemption reflect the director's profound debt to, and subsequent rejection of, neorealism. In the decade that followed he turned from objective observer to introspective dreamer. His films became increasingly personal in subject matter and extravagant in style. In 1956 he was a master director: within a few years he was an international superstar.

After the release of *The Nights of Cabiria*, Fellini wrote *Fortunella* (1958), a screenplay, for the director Eduardo De Filippo, and considered directing either an adaptation of Casanova's *Memoirs* or *Moraldo in the City*. He rejected both but Moraldo was the inspiration for the character of Marcello in *La dolce vita* (1960), which was co-written with Pinelli, Flaiano and Brunello Rondi. A masterly depiction of the kind of decadence and sin found more commonly in the films of Cecil B. DeMille, *La dolce vita* tells the satirical story of a young man who arrives in Rome from the provinces to follow a career in journalism. Principal photography on the picture, which was shot in Totalscope, lasted for over five months. At the end of the shoot Fellini was left with 56 hours of film. A feature just under three hours long was released in February 1960. The film secured Fellini's reputation as an *auteur* of the highest order.

In *Il bidone* and *The Nights of Cabiria*, Fellini depicted the individual's quest for rebirth. With this new film, he looks at society's collective need for such regeneration. In its stupendous opening scene, a helicopter dangles a statue of Christ, arms raised, overlooking the city below him. Set over seven days and nights, the film follows cynical and world-weary gossip journalist Marcello Rubini (Marcello Mastroianni) on a rake's progress through Rome. To snare the best scoops, Marcello spends his time prying among the various cafés and bars on Rome's via Veneto, a high-profile road cluttered with the city's aspiring glitterati. Bored of his profession, and harbouring the desire to become a serious writer, Marcello seeks solace in casual sexual encounters. His first conquest is Maddalena (Anouk Aimée), who he meets in a nightclub and beds in a prostitute's apartment.

For Marcello, juggling sexual relationships is more difficult than his day job. He returns home to find his scorned mistress suffering from the after-effects of a botched suicide attempt. After he dumps her at the local hospital, Marcello eyes

Still from 'La dolce vita' (1960)
Sylvia (Anita Ekberg) represents a pure uninhibited sexuality in contrast to Marcello's spiritual impotence.

"I feel that decadence is indispensable to rebirth."
Federico Fellini [21]

Still from 'La dolce vita' (1960)
The Christ figure being carried over Rome in the
opening sequence prefigures the godless film to
come. Symbolically, Marcello Rubini is in the
pursuing helicopter.

ABOVE
Still from 'La dolce vita' (1960)
A fake miracle is turned into a media circus.
Religious icons and rituals are repeatedly shown
to be meaningless to the modern Romans.

PAGE 76
On the set of 'La dolce vita' (1960)
Federico Fellini shows Anita Ekberg how to
disembark from an aeroplane like a movie star.

PAGE 77
Still from 'La dolce vita' (1960)
A media frenzy accompanies Sylvia wherever
she goes.

dazzling blonde actress Sylvia (Anita Ekberg). After attending a press conference with the bombshell he escorts her through Rome. The evening results in a kiss in the Trevi Fountain and a punch-up with Sylvia's fiancé at her hotel. Further excursions follow. Marcello visits an intellectual gathering held by his friend Steiner and is called out to Terni to report on an alleged religious miracle. He dines with his father and then finds himself at an aristocrat's house party outside Rome. The next day brings a debauched orgy at the home of a movie producer. Marcello presides over the socialite-stuffed gathering and witnesses a striptease performance by a newly divorced woman. The news then arrives that Steiner has murdered himself and his two children. As dawn breaks, Marcello emerges bleary-eyed on to the beach, where he is confronted with two symbolic images. A washed up sea monster sprawled on the sand reflects his own degenerated state. Some distance away, he observes a young girl representing purity and innocence. He tries to communicate with the girl but cannot make himself heard. He is left, like *La strada*'s Zampanò, alone on the beach.

La dolce vita introduced Mastroianni and Ekberg to an international audience. The film's one-time producer Dino de Laurentiis had initially recommended Paul Newman for the lead role of the gossip columnist. Fellini refused on the grounds that Newman was the kind of glamorous star Marcello would chase along the via Veneto. In Newman's place, he cast seasoned stage actor Mastroianni, who he had met in 1948 when the actor appeared alongside Masina in a production of Leo Ferrero's *Angelica*. Although the film doesn't mark the actor's screen debut – he'd appeared previously in Luchino Visconti's 1957 classic *Le notti bianche* (*White Nights*) – it earned him considerable critical acclaim and public attention. In the years that followed *La dolce vita*'s release, he would become known as 'Il Bel Marcello' in Italy. With later films such as *Divorzio all'italiana* (*Divorce – Italian Style*, 1961) Mastroianni became Italy's most internationally famous actor. He was recognised as Fellini's cinematic alter ego, sharing a working relationship with the director similar to that between François Truffaut and Jean-Pierre Léaud. Mastroianni's status as a surrogate Fellini was highlighted in *La dolce vita* by Marcello's profession – Fellini had worked as a journalist in his early days in Rome.

Alongside Mastroianni, Fellini cast Anita Ekberg, a former Miss Sweden and a striking 'sweater girl' with the kind of full fantasy figure he liked to sketch. Fellini first spied Ekberg in photos of her dancing in the Trevi Fountain in *Tempo illustrato*. She had previously appeared with Audrey Hepburn and Henry Fonda in King Vidor's flawed adaptation of *War and Peace*, filmed in Rome and released in 1956. Although she went on to star in several of Fellini's later films, Ekberg would forever be remembered for her appearance in *La dolce vita*. In conversation with Giovanni Grazzini, Fellini himself commented, "Twenty-five years after the film, its title, its image are still inseparable from Anita."[9]

Fellini researched the world depicted in *La dolce vita* during the summer of 1958. He became a regular at the cafés along the via Veneto, learning the tricks of the trade from its hordes of photographer-reporters. Famously, he chose to recreate the street at Cinecittà at the expense of his own percentage of the film's profits. Designer Piero Gherardi built him a long strip of via Veneto on Cinecittà's number 5 stage. One of more than eighty sets constructed for the film, this strip was almost an exact replica of the original. The only major difference was that Gherardi's street was flat, while the real via Veneto had a slope.

ABOVE
On the set of 'La dolce vita' (1960)
Filming the most famous scene in the film at the Trevi Fountain, when Marcello realises that Sylvia is the only pure person he knows.

RIGHT
On the set of 'La dolce vita' (1960)
Fellini assists Anita Ekberg out of the Trevi Fountain.

ABOVE
Still from 'La dolce vita' (1960)
Marcello Rubini (Marcello Mastroianni) and
Sylvia are captured by the paparazzi. Film stars
and other celebrities are the new gods of Rome.

LEFT
On the set of 'La dolce vita' (1960)
Fellini looks on as Anita Ekberg plays with a
kitten.

La dolce vita's international reception could not have been predicted. It swiftly entered into the public's consciousness. The kind of turtleneck sweater favoured by the stars of the film became known as a 'dolce vita.' The surname of the principal photographer, Paparazzo, became the accepted name for any gossip photographer, more recognisable in its plural of 'paparazzi.' 'Felliniesque' became a commonplace phrase. National monuments such as the Trevi Fountain became instantly synonymous with the film and its stars, attracting visitors from all over the world. When Mastroianni died over 30 years later, the fountain was symbolically switched off and draped in black as a tribute.

The film was a cause célèbre, quickly gaining a reputation as a contentious, controversial feature that demanded a reaction from all quarters. The press and the Catholic Church were quick to make their voices heard. One Italian newspaper called the film 'This Disgusting Life,' while the Church condemned it as pornographic. Some threatened the director and anyone who saw the film with excommunication. Right-wing extremists labelled it immoral and even called for Fellini's arrest. After one screening in Milan, a member of the audience spat in the director's face. Fellini's own mother couldn't understand why he'd made such a picture. Such powerful reactions helped turn *La dolce vita* into an instant box-office smash, breaking all previous records in Italy and allowing Fellini to set up his own production company, which he named Federiz. The film enjoyed considerable critical success, becoming the accepted benchmark of art cinema. Fellini was awarded the Palme d'Or at Cannes and became the first foreign film-maker to be nominated in the Best Director category at the Oscars. He lost but Piero Gherardi won Best Costume Design.

Still from 'La dolce vita' (1960)
Nadia (Nadia Gray) celebrates her divorce by stripping for her friends.

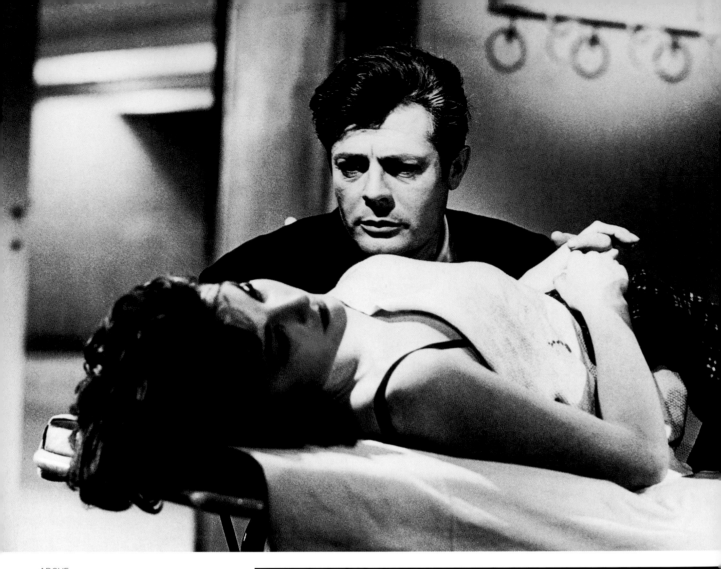

ABOVE
Still from 'La dolce vita' (1960)
Marcello was making love to heiress Maddalena, whilst his jealous girlfriend Emma (Yvonne Fourneaux) attempted suicide.

RIGHT
Still from 'La dolce vita' (1960)
The conspicuous wealth of the characters – sports cars, parties, villas, furs – is a fleeting distraction from the emptiness they feel. The characters are trying to deny their anguish and alienation.

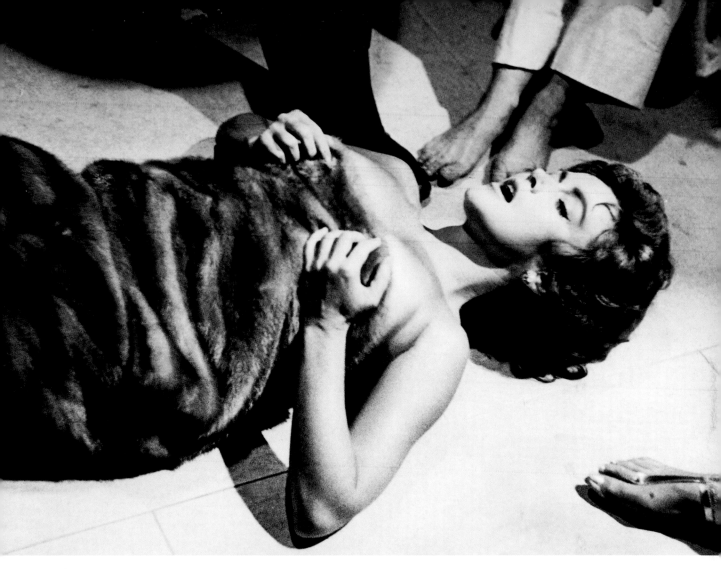

ABOVE
Still from 'La dolce vita' (1960)
Nadia's striptease reaches its climax.

LEFT
Still from 'La dolce vita' (1960)
Resigned to a soulless life, Marcello joins the orgy.

PAGES 86/87
Still from 'La dolce vita' (1960)
Marcello's anguish is evident when a monster fish is beached. The beach is where Fellini's characters must decide whether they face reality or live in a dream world.

Fellini followed up his longest feature yet with another contribution to an omnibus film. The *Boccaccio '70* project, originally designed as an updated alternative to the *Decameron*, was produced by Carlo Ponti and co-ordinated by Cesare Zavattini. The compilation contained four shorts. Contributing episodes alongside Fellini were Luchino Visconti (*Il lavoro*), Vittorio De Sica (*La riffa*) and Mario Monicelli (*Renzo e Luciana*). Together, this quartet of films, with a combined running time of three and a half hours, became something of a doctrine against censorship. In 1960, Visconti's epic family study *Rocco e i suoi fratelli* (*Rocco and his Brothers*) had come under fire for its homosexual content. His *Il lavoro*, starring Romy Schneider and Thomas Milian, took call girls as its subject matter. Fellini's Technicolor short, *Le tentazioni del dottor Antonio* (*The Temptations of Doctor Antonio,* 1962), written in just two weeks, can be read as a response to the reactions met by *La dolce vita*. It examines the futility of attempting to repress one's sexual instincts.

The film follows the misfortunes of its titular hero (Peppino De Filippo), a moral crusader who finds himself helplessly attracted to a big-breasted billboard model (Anita Ekberg). The model features predominantly in a ludicrously loaded advertising poster for milk. At first the poster angers the straight-laced doctor who insists on its removal and tries to obscure the image by projecting ink over its surface. His travails fail to remove the image and the doctor subsequently slips into a fantasy in which he gives in to the model's ample charms. He awakes sprawled over the billboard and is taken away in an ambulance.

By satirising the advertising world in this humorous short, Fellini returned to his early work for *Marc'Aurelio*, for which he had written a series of parodies under the title *Il raccontino pubblicitario* (*The Advertising Story*). These early pieces satirised the ludicrous claims of the commercials of the day. Advertising annoyed him throughout his career. With the rise of television, he grew to resent the effect that commercial breaks had on televised feature films, especially his own. He returned to this theme in *Ginger and Fred* and *Intervista* (*Inter-*

ABOVE
Still from 'The Temptations of Doctor Antonio' (1962)
Moral hypocrite Doctor Antonio Mazzuolo (Peppino De Filippo) is tempted by Anita (Anita Ekberg), the girl on the billboard made flesh.

RIGHT
Still from 'The Temptations of Doctor Antonio' (1962)
Doctor Mazzuolo spouts his rhetoric to boy scouts as the offending billboard is erected.

view, 1988) yet directed advertising spots himself in 1984, for Barilla and Campari.

Antonio's obsession with the billboard vamp recalls Checco's infatuation with Liliana in *Variety Lights*, not least because the same actor, Peppino De Filippo, plays the lead in both. *The Temptations of Doctor Antonio* is notable principally for De Filippo's assured comic performance in the lead role. It remains, however, a slight piece, and one that wasn't particularly well received at the time. In a review for the influential French journal *Cahiers du cinéma*, Jean Douchet went so far as to label it 'a complete disaster.'[10] Like Fellini's flamboyant sketches, many found it too coarse and gratuitous, rejecting it as a schoolboy fantasy and nothing more. Most critics singled out Visconti's piece as the compilation's most rewarding.

Still from 'The Temptations of Doctor Antonio' (1962)
Anita strips for Doctor Mazzuolo but his resolve remains firm and he kills her. Anita represents the seduction of the media, and Doctor Mazzuolo the hypocrisy of critics.

Fellini, as ever, carried on regardless. He even found his next feature film moving into production before he had a clear-cut idea about its plot. As he told Giovanni Grazzini, he had only a "vague confused desire to create the portrait of a man on a certain day of his life."[11] Despite receiving only vague information about the project, cast and crew signed up for the film that would become *8 1/2* and awaited more detailed information. Little did they know their *maestro* was experiencing an acute crisis of confidence. As the starting date for the shoot approached, Fellini feared that he had lost hold of the film. On the set one evening, he began an awkward letter to his Milanese producer, Angelo Rizzoli, explaining that he would be unable to direct the feature. As he persevered with this difficult task he was disturbed by the arrival of a crew member, announcing that it was the birthday of one of the machinists. Fellini attended the gathering outside where everyone was in high spirits. When someone raised a glass to the director, and to the film they were about to make, Fellini felt sick to his stomach. He shied away from the group and retired to the garden to reflect on his dilemma. Suddenly, the solution suggested itself. "I got straight to the heart of the film," he told Grazzini. "I would narrate everything that had been happening to me. I would make a film telling the story of a director who no longer knows what film he wanted to make."[12]

With a message pasted on his camera that read, 'Remember that this is a comic film,' Fellini began to shoot his intricate portrait of a paralysed artist in May 1962. He wouldn't wrap the feature until mid-October. The film was shot during a strike held by the local film laboratories, which meant that Fellini filmed material for four months without seeing the rushes. Sets came and went, and actors arrived, played their parts and left, all before Fellini could watch a minute of the film he was directing. At the end of filming he spent three days in a projection room to witness the fruits of the shoot.

The film opens with a nightmare. A famous director, Guido Anselmi (Mastroianni), is trapped in a traffic jam, struggling to get out of his car. He eventually succeeds, rising out of the car and floating away to freedom, only to be rudely dragged back to earth seconds later. This astonishing opening sequence is one of Guido's fantasies. Overworked and under pressure, the director checks into a health resort where he is to undergo a cure. As he tries to recuperate in the retreat's attractive grounds, he is bombarded with requests and demands from those working on his new project, a science fiction film set in a future threatened by thermonuclear war. To add to these difficulties, he must balance his relationships with his married mistress Carla (Sandra Milo) and his perceptive wife Luisa (Anouk Aimée). As he juggles both partners he is also entranced by the intermittent appearance of a mysterious vision of beauty (Claudia Cardinale).

Far from making a recovery, Guido comes under increasing levels of stress. This anguish provokes an escalation of his dream life and a preoccupation with his childhood. Day to day incidents at the resort subsequently trigger a series of memories. As a child, he remembers paying a mysterious woman named Saraghina to dance the Rumba for him on the beach. (The incident amounts to a semi-titillating yet strangely beautiful prowl around the sand.) He also recalls being bathed in wine by a group of maids. Coupled with such memories are a number of outrageous fantasies presenting metaphors for his current state. In one he is a circus master keeping his acquaintances at bay; in another he rules

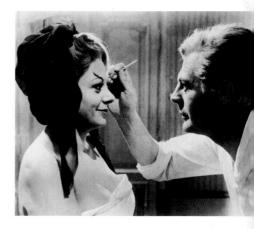

ABOVE
Still from '8 1/2' (1963)
Guido and his vulgar lover Carla (Sandra Milo) play around as a prelude to their lovemaking.

OPPOSITE
Still from '8 1/2' (1963)
Guido Anselmi (Marcello Mastroianni) in the opening traffic jam scene. This dream makes it explicit that the whole film takes place in Guido's mind, and also that he wants to escape his responsibilities.

PAGES 92/93
On the set of '8 1/2' (1963)
Fellini shows Marcello Mastroianni and Sandra Milo how he wants them to make love.

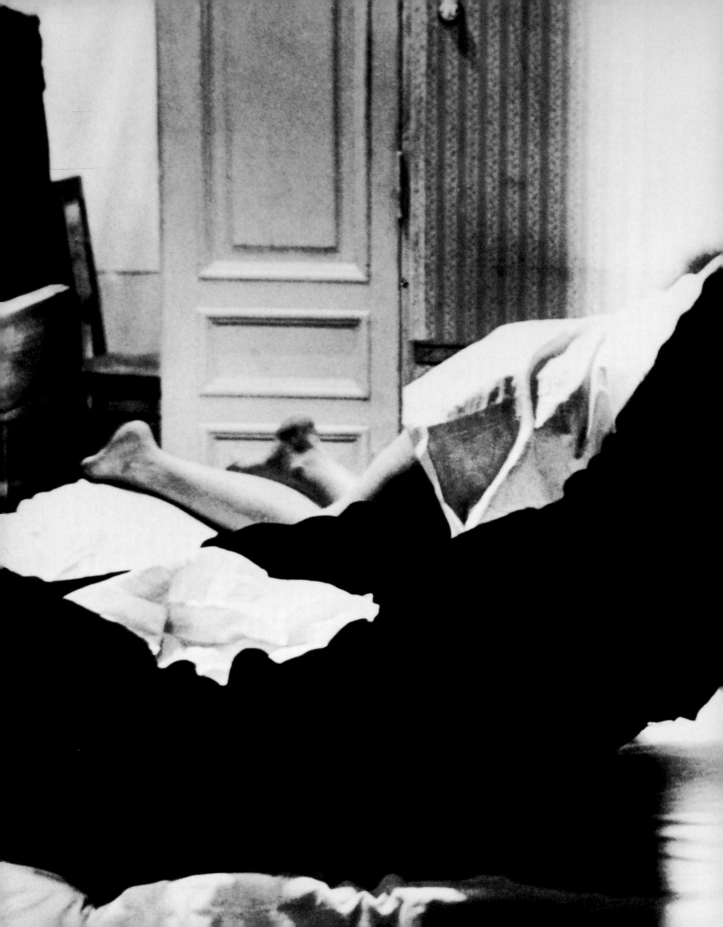

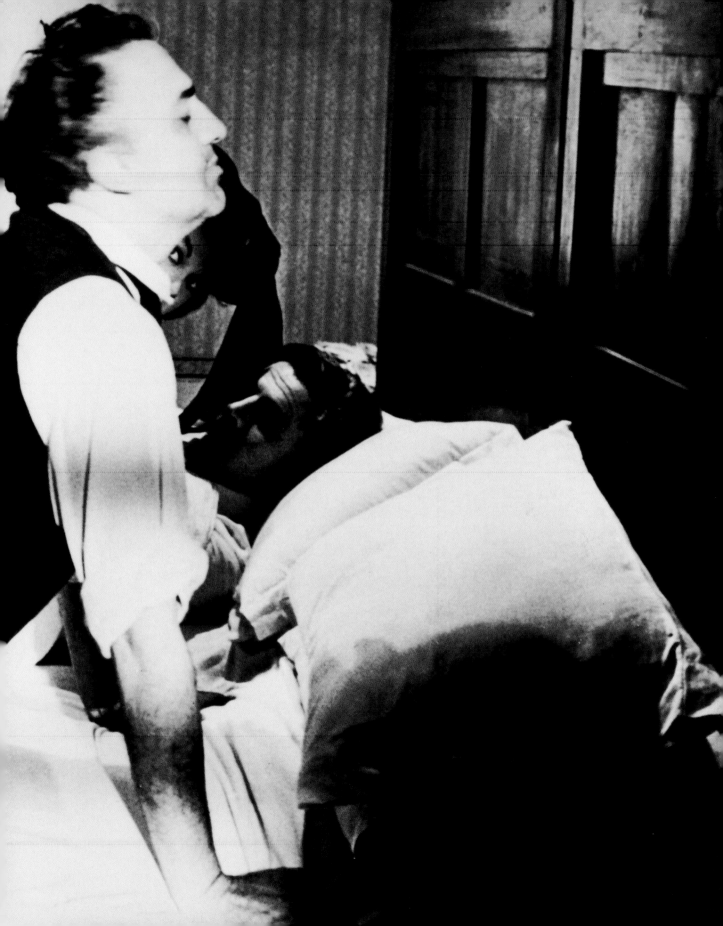

a fantastical harem. And in between the dreams comes the recurring question: will his new film ever see the light of day?

That Fellini should decide to direct a film about film-making made perfect sense. After all, he set his first films against the worlds he was familiar with. *8 1/2* would become recognised as the director's definitive ode to the cinema, fitting neatly into that enticing subgenre – the film about film-making. Films about films were by no means new in 1963. *The Bad and the Beautiful* (1952) and *Singin' in the Rain* (1952) were released some ten years earlier. However, both *8 1/2* and Jean-Luc Godard's *Le Mépris* (*Contempt*, 1963) directly influenced a specific new type of metafictional cinema focusing on the director's creative dilemmas. The influence of Fellini's picture can be seen in François Truffaut's *La Nuit américaine* (*Day for Night*, 1973), Woody Allen's *Stardust Memories* (1980), Christopher Guest's *The Big Picture* (1988) and Roman Coppola's *CQ* (2001). Unusually, and unlike most of the aforementioned features, we never see the film within the film in *8 1/2*. Furthermore, as opposed to films like *The Bad and the Beautiful* and *La Nuit américaine*, we learn very little about the film industry from it.

Fellini made no efforts to hide the autobiographical nature of his new picture. This is immediately suggested by its title, chosen because it represents film number eight and a half in his career thus far. (He counted the six features he had directed on his own, added the new one, then added on half a point for each of the three features he had co-directed: *Variety Lights*, *Love in the City* and *Boccaccio '70*.) In *8 1/2* he draws on his experiences in the film industry, focusing in particular on his relationships with cast, crew and producers. The film cemented Mastroianni's reputation as Fellini's alter ego. He plays a similarly aged director struggling to approach his follow-up to a huge success. He also dresses like Fellini, sporting a black suit with accompanying hat. Guido's filmmaking habits are akin to Fellini's. He plays his cards close to his chest, refusing to impart information to his cast and crew. We constantly see him surrounded by the kind of actors' mugshots that cluttered up Fellini's office. At one point, Guido is even referred to as "maestro." Fellini described himself as a ringmaster, and in one of the film's more famous scenes Guido is literally imagined as such a character.

While Guido's exterior world reflects Fellini the film-maker's professional life, his interior world depicts episodes from Fellini's personal life as a child. The scene in which a young Guido is bathed in wine and prepared for bed was based on a childhood memory, as is the Saraghina episode. The real-life Saraghina, a large and mysterious woman who lived in isolation on the beach, flashed her private parts to an eight-year-old Fellini and his friends for a small sum of money. More recent elements from Fellini's private life also enter the film, such as his troubled relationship with his father, who died of a heart attack in 1956. (Urbano Fellini appears to have also been the model for Marcello's father in *La dolce vita*. Annibale Ninchi plays the role of the father in both films.)

In *8 1/2* Fellini satirises the critics' reception of his work in general – and *La dolce vita* in particular – just as he had done in *The Temptations of Doctor Antonio*. Early on, the doctor sarcastically enquires of him, "What are you working on now? Another film without hope?" Both his plots and his characters are torn to shreds and his work is condemned as a "squalid catalogue of mistakes." Fellini

ABOVE
Still from '8 1/2' (1963)
Fellini uses dramatic lighting to emphasise the dancing shadows of Gloria (Barbara Steele) and Mario (Mario Pisu).

OPPOSITE
Still from '8 1/2' (1963)
Guido is directing a film, but he does not know what it is about. His mind is constantly distracted by events around him and from his past. He is trying to avoid the weight of his responsibilities.

Still from '8 1/2' (1963)
Guido seeks answers from the Cardinal, who is visiting the spa Guido is staying at. The meeting proves fruitless.

safeguards himself against future criticism of his work by pre-empting it in this manner. At the same time he also has his revenge on the critics with a fantasy scene that sees the critic Daumier strung up and hung in the movie theatre.

8 1/2 marked another advance in style and structure. Its ambitious nature is reflected by Guido's declaration that "Everything happens in my film. I'm going to put everything in." The film follows a loose narrative based around Guido's stay at the resort yet also moves freely in and out of the character's assorted dreams and memories. As such, the film boasts a considerably more complex temporal structure than *La dolce vita*, which presented a largely linear series of events. While *8 1/2* also presents a series of sequences, or frescoes, here they are linked within Guido's consciousness. This means there are three major temporal 'locations' in the film: the present day, the past and Guido's fantasy world. *8 1/2* consequently requires a more active viewer than most pictures. The film's producers – and even some of the stars – feared it would be too inaccessible for mainstream audiences. To make the film itself easier to understand,

the dream sequences were set in colour – against Fellini's will – in prints sent to the provinces.

8 1/2 is a collaborative triumph. The screenplay, co-written with Pinelli, Flaiano and Rondi, is full of little truths about relationships, religion, work and films. The crisp cinematography has an austere quality and there is complex use of both diegetic and non-diegetic sound. The marvellously varied score features Rota's original music for the Cordovox organ (previously used on *La dolce vita*) and music from Wagner and Tchaikovsky. The film was screened out of competition at Cannes in May 1963 and was enthusiastically received. Critics quickly extracted a wealth of presumed artistic influences, such as Marcel Proust's *A la recherche du temps perdu*, James Joyce's *Ulysses* and Alain Resnais' *L'Année dernière à Marienbad (Last Year at Marienbad*, 1961). Fellini, who often felt himself to be intellectually inferior, claimed never to have seen or read the majority of such works. One undeniable influence, however, was the groundbreaking research of Carl Gustav Jung into the collective unconscious.

ABOVE
Still from '8 1/2' (1963)
Claudia (Claudia Cardinale) is Guido's dream image of the ideal woman.

PAGES 98/99
Still from '8 1/2' (1963)
Guido retreats into a dream of his ideal harem, which includes all the women who have influenced his life and dreams. Here he is trying to hold La Saraghina (Edra Gale) at bay.

At the Oscars, Gherardi won another award for Best Costume Design and Fellini received his third statuette for Best Foreign Language Picture. It would prove to be Fellini's own personal favourite of his films and has been particularly popular with other directors over the 40 years since its release. Bob Fosse directed both a feature film (*All That Jazz*, 1979) and a Broadway musical (*Nine*, first performed in 1981) influenced by *8 1/2*.

Pauline Kael gave a perceptive review of Fellini's *8 1/2*, commenting, "When a satire on big, expensive movies is itself a big, expensive movie, how can we distinguish it from its target? When a man makes himself the butt of his own joke, we may feel too uncomfortable to laugh." Her assessment of the film-maker's dilemma, given in the same broadcast, was also right on the money. "A movie director has two 'worst' enemies: commercial failure and commercial success. After a failure, he has a difficult time raising money for his next film; after a success, his next must be bigger and 'better.'"[13] Sure enough, *8 1/2*'s runaway success raised the stakes for Fellini's next production. The director was already aware of a disquieting pattern in his work that saw the follow-ups to hugely popular and critically lauded films such as *La strada* and *La dolce vita* mercilessly panned. *Il bidone* and *Boccaccio '70* had also proved box-office poison. All the more reason, then, to approach his next project with caution.

"The best part of the day is when I go to bed. I go to sleep and the fête begins."

Federico Fellini[23]

OPPOSITE
Still from '8 1/2' (1963)
The spacecraft set is where Guido turns all his dreams into reality, and puts them into his film.

PAGES 102/103
Still from '8 1/2' (1963)
Fellini often compared his role as film director with that of a ringmaster. Here he makes the connection explicit.

Dreaming in Colour
1965–1970

Having dabbled (by demand) with colour in his *Boccaccio '70* episode, Fellini chose to shoot the follow-up to *8 1/2* in Technicolor. The fantastical *Juliet of the Spirits* was conceived as another vehicle for Masina, marking a return to Italian film-making for the actress who had broken the nation's hearts as Gelsomina. Fellini had been preparing the role of Giulietta ever since *La strada*. Of all the characters Masina portrayed in her husband's films, Fellini felt that this one represented her best.

Giulietta is a lady of leisure with a beautiful house, bourgeois lifestyle and successful husband (Mario Pisu). But all is not quite as it seems. When Giulietta overhears her other half whisper the name of another woman in his sleep, she grows suspicious and visits a fortune-teller for guidance. She then turns to a private eye, whom she hires to follow her husband, and also seeks companionship from her neighbour Susy (Sandra Milo), a middle-aged hedonist who denies herself nothing and encourages sexual exploration. When she receives a report from the PI confirming her suspicions, Giulietta is distraught. Susy invites her to attend an outlandish orgy at her villa. Giulietta acquiesces, but she is unable to go through with an infidelity of her own. Increasingly troubled by bad dreams, mysterious voices, nightmarish visions and unhappy memories of her Catholic upbringing, Giulietta finds herself in the throes of an identity crisis. Again, she seeks understanding through others, visiting first a psychiatrist and then her husband's mistress. She eventually looks within herself for answers and, at the end of the film, emerges from her house and walks away to freedom.

Juliet of the Spirits is regarded as a female companion piece to *8 1/2*, because both Giulietta and Guido undergo a crisis that forces them to confront their fears. Upon its release, Fellini drew a comparison between Giulietta and Cabiria, explaining that both battle to understand religion, love and mysticism. For the tale of the superstitious Giulietta he attended séances, visited numerous mediums and tarot card readers, and drew on his broad knowledge of the occult. For both Guido and Giulietta, the past continually crystallises on the present. The exploration of Giulietta's dream life highlights Fellini's fascination with Jungian psychology and psychoanalysis – an interest sparked by a visit to Jungian analyst Ernst Bernhard during *La dolce vita*. During their "psychological dialogues" Bernhard

OPPOSITE
Still from 'Fellini's Satyricon' (1969)
Encolpio must face the Minotaur (Luigi Montefiori) to win Ariadne. He emerges impotent from the labyrinth (a metaphor for the unconscious mind). We then follow him as he seeks a cure.

PAGES 106/107
Still from 'Juliet of the Spirits' (1965)
One of Giulietta's dreams. Since 'I vitelloni' Fellini had regularly featured beaches as symbolic places where characters attain self-realisation.

"Ernst Bernhard, the Jungian psychoanalyst, … made me grasp that our dream life is no less important than our waking life, especially for the artist."

Federico Fellini

ABOVE
Still from 'Juliet of the Spirits' (1965)
The uninhibited Susy (Sandra Milo) is a
projection of Giulietta's (Giulietta Masina)
repressed libido.

RIGHT
Still from 'Juliet of the Spirits' (1965)
Giulietta performs the rituals of being married
to a successful man and does not know how to
react when she finds out he is having an affair.

ABOVE & LEFT
Stills from 'Juliet of the Spirits' (1965)
The spirits Giulietta sees are reflections of her inner fears and desires.

PAGES 110/111
On the set of 'Juliet of the Spirits' (1965)
In this Jungian journey into a woman's subconscious, Fellini turned his wildest fantasies into reality. Here Fanny (Sandra Milo) prepares to elope with Giulietta's grandfather in a circus plane.

encouraged the director to keep the sketch diary of his dreams from which later projects would emerge.

With Giulietta's dream life given predominance throughout the film, it seems fitting that Fellini chose to direct the feature in colour. In doing so, he allowed the imaginations of Piero Gherardi and Gianni di Venanzo to run riot. Together the pair created a lurid, artificial fantasy world not unlike that seen in *The Wizard of Oz* (1939). The film's opulent palette marks it out as a product of those psychedelic times. In the year before *Juliet of the Spirits'* release two other films had embraced colour in a similarly enthusiastic manner: Jacques Demy's pastel-hued musical *Les Parapluies de Cherbourg* (*The Umbrellas of Cherbourg*, 1964) and Antonioni's portrait of alienation *Il deserto rosso* (*The Red Desert*, 1964). Colour is used throughout in an intelligent fashion, particularly for costume design. Giulietta mostly wears white – a sign of her innocence and fragility. In the orgy scene she appears in a bright red outfit, which represents her sudden desire to be sensual and passionate.

Like *La dolce vita*, the film was designed to work through a series of stunning visual sequences, rather than relying on a traditional narrative. Such an episodic, sketch-driven nature displays the influence of both comic strips and music hall routines on Fellini's work. He was trying to move from a prose narrative to poetry, eschewing traditional narrative demands en route. The public were unconvinced by such poetic aspirations and were not keen to see Masina play a part that marked such a stark contrast from her turns as Gelsomina and Cabiria. The film's cool public reception hurt Fellini. Worse still was the fact that due to various tensions during filming, he had fallen out with several key collaborators. Due to a quarrel, Gherardi, whose hallucinogenic and sugary set design had been singled out in most reviews of the film, would never work with the director again. The same thing happened with Flaiano. Masina, meanwhile, was exhausted from her experience on the film.

Still from 'Juliet of the Spirits' (1965)
Fellini's longtime collaborator Piero Gherardi designed the lavish sets and costumes.

With *Juliet of the Spirits* completed, Fellini decided to direct a picture about a
man who apparently avoids death only to realise some time later that he is in
fact deceased. Fellini spent most of 1966 preparing the screenplay of *Il viaggio
di G. Mastorna* with 60-year-old novelist Dino Buzzati. Producer Dino de Laurentiis paid for set construction at Dinocittà, his newly built studio complex on via
Pontina. As Fellini struggled with the casting, production costs began to spiral out
of control and he suffered a physical collapse. He was taken to hospital in April
1967 and sent to a villa in Manzania, where he remained for some time. *Mastorna*
was laid to rest. While Fellini would occasionally return to the script later, the
film never saw the light of day. A comic-strip version drawn by Milo Manara
appeared in 1992 in the monthly magazine *Il grifo*.

Until the forced period of inactivity following his collapse, Fellini had kept to
a hectic and incredibly productive working schedule. His '8 1/2' films were made
over an intense 13-year period that had also seen his involvement with seven
screenplays for other directors. The break from film-making gave the director
time to reassess his personal and professional life. He revisited Rimini, wrote an
autobiographical essay on his childhood and began to consider other projects.
The first of these to materialise was *Toby Dammit*, a dark contribution to an
uneven compilation film, *Tre passi nel delirio* (*Spirits of the Dead*, 1968). The
brainchild of French producer Raymond Eger, this collection was designed as

a tribute to Edgar Allan Poe. It consisted of a number of episodes based on the famed American author's short stories. Eger approached a number of directors for the project, including Luchino Visconti, Orson Welles and Joseph Losey, before eventually deciding on the film's line-up. To accompany Fellini he selected two film-makers associated with the French New Wave: Roger Vadim and Louis Malle.

Spirits of the Dead is a rather tedious triptych. Vadim's Metzengerstein stars Jane Fonda as a capricious countess who falls for her cousin (played, eerily, by Peter Fonda). Malle's doppelgänger drama William Wilson is narrated by Alain Delon, who plays the malicious and self-destructive Wilson, haunted by his double throughout his life. Toby Dammit is the only modern adaptation. The film stars Terence Stamp as the depressed and drug-addled titular actor. Subdued, dishevelled and made up to look like a modern-day Poe, Dammit arrives in Rome to appear in a "Catholic western" influenced by the unlikely trio of Dreyer, Pasolini and Ford. He is taken to a TV studio for an interview, then to a glitzy ceremony. Troubled by recurrent visions of a young girl playing with a ball – an image he equates with the devil – Dammit leaves the ceremony and races away in a new Ferrari. Arriving at the site of a collapsed bridge, he spies the young girl on the other side and attempts to cross. In doing so he fails to spot a steel wire stretched across the road and is swiftly decapitated. The closing image has the girl leave her ball and take Dammit's head with her instead.

Despite never being an avid reader (his preference was for Simenon thrillers and Bradbury adventures), Fellini had been fascinated by Poe since childhood. As a youth he wanted to look like the brooding author. Toby Dammit is a loose adaptation of the little-known story Never Bet the Devil Your Head. Fellini co-wrote the script with Bernardino Zapponi, another veteran from Marc'Aurelio. The Tell-Tale Heart and The Premature Burial were initially considered for the adaptation (Fellini rejecting the former, producers rejecting the latter) before the final tale was agreed upon. In the film little remains from Poe's story except the hero's name and his decapitation. Unlike Bertolucci (Il conformista/The Conformist, 1970) and Pasolini (Oedipus Rex, 1967), the maestro traditionally shied away from adapting literary material for the big screen. He would later confess that he didn't read Poe's original story until after the film was completed.

Toby Dammit reveals several key Fellinian concerns. The arrival of an international star bombarded by photographers is reminiscent of La dolce vita. The satirical presentation of an artificial TV chat show, complete with canned laughter, pre-empts Ginger and Fred. As Dammit, Stamp cuts a jaded and world-weary figure, occasionally reminiscent of Mastroianni's onscreen incarnations. His boast "I only live during the night" particularly recalls Marcello Rubini's lifestyle. The film's themes (solitude, celebrity, superstition) and images (the little girl, clowns, the streets of Rome) are also familiar. The style of shooting, however, represents a departure for the rarely ostentatious director, who utilises a number of unusual techniques to create a hallucinogenic Rome.

Still from 'Toby Dammit' (1968)
On the road to nowhere, Toby bets the Devil that he can jump a broken bridge with his sports car.

Fellini's next film would deliver a similarly infernal vision. While in Manzania recovering from pleurisy, Fellini reread the *Satyricon*, a sprawling collection of tales written by Petronius, one of Emperor Nero's advisers. He had considered the project since his days at *Marc'Aurelio*, when it was judged a possible vehicle for Aldo Fabrizi. His *Satyricon* is as idiosyncratic and personal an adaptation as *Toby Dammit*: this was the *Satyricon* as told by Fellini not Petronius. Two of Fellini's preoccupations of the time, hallucinogenic drugs and science fiction, shaped the look and feel of the film. He commented that he would examine ancient Rome as if he was making a documentary about Martians. In keeping with the sci-fi theme, he attempted to reflect the colour of Alexander Raymond's *Flash Gordon* comic strip, using various colour filters and different types of stock.

Fellini's Satyricon was shot between November 1968 and May 1969 – a time when experimentation, polysexuality and self-discovery were in vogue. The film is filled with the spirit of liberation, as celebrated by the hippy movement. Like the flower children of the 1960s, Fellini's hedonistic ancient Romans live for the moment, blissfully oblivious of the consequences of their actions. In *Fellini's Satyricon*, anything goes. The film primarily follows two adolescent Romans, Encolpio (Martin Potter) and Ascilto (Hiram Keller), who are kidnapped by a pirate and enslaved upon a boat. Once freed, they pursue various sexual conquests until Encolpio is captured and forced to fight a Minotaur. The incident brings about his impotence, displayed by his failed attempts at copulation with Ariadne. To solve the problem Encolpio first visits the Garden of Delights and then the mysterious Oenothea, who finally restores his virility. When Ascilto dies, Encolpio decides to board a ship for Africa. The film ends with him setting out on the journey.

La dolce vita in sandals, *Fellini's Satyricon* is a surrealist extravagance. Vicious and glorious in equal measure, it serves as an exposé of amorality and debauchery. (In *Le Nouvel observateur*, the critic Jean-Louis Bory went as far as to call the film "the contemplation of a steaming cess-pool."[14]) Both films offer a kaleidoscopic portrait of Rome, from the city's poor to its overwhelmingly prosperous. Like *La dolce vita*, *Fellini's Satyricon* is designed as a fresco critique of contemporary Roman society. For Fellini, the lives of the ancients are just as dissipated and filled with empty pursuits as those of the people who frequent the via Veneto. *Fellini's Satyricon* matches the earlier film's sense of ambition and was similarly criticised as undisciplined. This is partly because Fellini favours once more the picaresque structure and uses the original work's incomplete status to his advantage. Fellini's episodic film ends mid-sentence, like Petronius' book, and then Encolpio is transformed into a fresco with the other characters. *Fellini's Satyricon* has a cyclical nature, opening and closing with similar images, which Fellini had done before in *Il bidone* and *La strada*.

Satyricon's bored young characters, clinging desperately to their adolescence, are themselves not unlike the *vitelloni*. They go about their pleasures mechanically, resigned to their perversions. Consequently, the viewer gets as little satisfaction from the depraved escapades of these assorted rulers, scoundrels and rough trade as they do. Watching bad behaviour, critics remarked, was rarely this boring. For all its orgies, banquets, violence and sexual escapades, *Fellini's Satyricon* fails to titillate. Part of the reason lies in Fellini's original intention to make the film as a kind of documentary. Almost all the music is diegetic and the action is

Still from 'Fellini's Satyricon' (1969)
There are strange and exotic rituals throughout the film. This one takes place when Ascilto, Encolpio and Gitone are enslaved on the ship of proconsul Lica (Alain Cuny, left).

ABOVE
Still from 'Fellini's Satyricon' (1969)
In another ritual, the guests of the ex-slave Trimalchione wash before they take part in his lavish banquet.

PAGE 122
Still from 'Fellini's Satyricon' (1969)
Fellini always references the media in his work and in 'Satyricon' they are poets, oracles and mosaics. In one episode Ascilto and Encolpio abduct an albino hermaphrodite oracle.

PAGE 123
Still from 'Fellini's Satyricon' (1969)
Encolpio prepares to face the Minotaur.

Still from 'Fellini's Satyricon' (1969)
Fellini shows many forms of sexuality in the film. Sex is enjoyable, healing and comforting for the characters. Here Lica lies with Gitone.

shot in an unobtrusive style designed to prevent audience identification with the central characters, in contrast to *La dolce vita*. Yet the film fails as a documentary about ancient Rome. It is merely a laborious portrait of Fellini's own dream world.

Satyricon was Fellini's most expensive movie to date. The film used 90 sets, all of which were constructed at Cinecittà. It boasted a distinctive cast of 250 players, among them huge puffy women and near skeletal men. Fittingly, his bizarre, sensuous mosaic of life in ancient Rome received its American premiere after a rock concert at Madison Square Garden. According to Fellini, the film played to a crowd of 10,000 entwined hippies high on dope. As usual, it is easy to accuse the *maestro* of exaggeration. Nevertheless, the film reached its target audience

on release, when United Artists pitched it as a youth movie. The sheer originality of Fellini's spectacle of decadence was applauded in many reviews and brought him another Best Director Oscar nomination.

Still from 'Fellini's Satyricon' (1969)
After Trimalchione is too attentive to two male slaves, his wife Fortunata (Magali Noël, right) seeks revenge in the embrace of another woman.

PAGES 126/127
On the set of 'Fellini's Satyricon' (1969)
This is one of 90 magical sets designed by Danilo Donati for the production.

Fellini's initial experiences on the set of *Fellini's Satyricon* were recorded in *Block-notes di un regista* (*Fellini: A Director's Notebook*, 1969), an hour-long documentary for America's NBC television network. The film works as a brief tribute to the aborted *Mastorna* project, capturing for the sake of posterity the abandoned cathedral set in its opening minutes. The film's informal documentary nature makes it something of a precursor to later works such as *Intervista* and *Roma*, and to his next immediate project, *The Clowns*.

An affectionate and enjoyable mosaic about the world of the circus, *The Clowns* comprises three sections. It opens with a young child, presumably Fellini, awakening to the sound of noise outside. Seeing a circus tent, he leaves his room and, dressed in his sailor suit, enters the big top. A series of amazing feats are introduced with rhetoric ("Anyone with a weak heart had better leave") worthy of Zampanò. Knives are thrown at a woman in an exotic costume, performers wrestle to the sound of Wagner and a mermaid is wheeled out. Before long, clowns appear, bashing each other with hammers and firing a cannon. The clowns frighten the boy, their "twisted drunken masks" and "enigmatic expressions" reminding him of everyday figures from his village.

The next section commences with Fellini dictating a query to his scriptgirl ("The clowns of my childhood – where are they today?") and setting off to answer the question with a film crew in tow. At an Italian circus they bump into Anita Ekberg and see two clowns perform. In Paris they visit the birthplace of the Cirque d'Hiver, track down elderly clowns and visit a circus historian. The film's final act takes place entirely in the circus ring, as Fellini puts on a show for the viewer. Clowns inflict a series of comically violent pranks upon one another and a procession follows, culminating in a giant champagne bottle popping its cork and a lone clown swinging high above the celebrations. In the closing scene, two clowns play the trumpet in the spotlight of an empty arena.

One of Fellini's childhood ambitions was to be able to make people laugh. As a film-maker he compared his role on set to that of a ringleader or circus master. His world is one of downtrodden individuals who manage to raise a smile at their sorry lot in life. As such, clowns – whether literal or not – appear throughout his work. The spectacle of the circus influenced Fellini's films from his very first, *Variety Lights*. By 1970, the clown's visage, a tragicomic tone, closing procession and characters dangling in mid-air or caught in the spotlight had long been associated with Fellini's cinema. His long-term fascination with the marginal figure of the clown had developed into his interest in the freakish and grotesque, as displayed in *Fellini's Satyricon*. The closing scene of that earlier film, in which Encolpio is transformed into a fresco, is reversed in *The Clowns* when a photograph of three performers comes to life. As in *Satyricon*, Fellini again uses the atmospherics of the comic strip in the film's mise en scène. The opening sequence recalls Winsor McCay's *Little Nemo in Slumberland*.

Like the pseudo-documentaries *Roma* and *Intervista*, *The Clowns* is a film with many layers. Ostensibly, it is a documentary following a crew making a documentary. However, as in *8 1/2* we never see the 'film within the film' because Fellini's interest is once more in the work-in-progress. At times, the inept crew behave like clowns, and at the end of the film Fellini plays the role of circus director himself. Francesco Dorigo neatly summed up the director's

ABOVE
Still from 'The Clowns' (1970)
The clown is sad about life and playful with death. He appears childlike but is the father of dreams. The clown is an important symbol in the cinema of Federico Fellini.

OPPOSITE
Federico Fellini (c. 1969)
Fellini's first job was as a cartoonist and he never stopped drawing. He even drew cartoons on his scripts. Here Fellini designs the costumes and makeup for 'The Clowns.'

ABOVE
On the set of 'The Clowns' (1970)
Federico Fellini is both the ringmaster and director.

RIGHT
On the set of 'The Clowns' (1970)
Fellini in serious discussion with a clown.

affinity with the film's performers in *Il piccolo* when he wrote that *The Clowns* 'has the final touch of a director who never gives in to easy sentimentalism, but rather, when he sees that a tear is welling, quickly turns it into a subdued laugh.'[15]

On the set of 'The Clowns' (1970)
Fellini liked to show his performers how to play a scene rather than explain it verbally.

"It is likely that if the cinema had not existed, if I had not met Rossellini and if the circus were still a show that had a present-day life of its own, I should have liked to be the director of a big circus."

Federico Fellini [21]

Sex, the City & Snàporaz
1972–1981

By the 1970s, Fellini's work had long reflected the director's continued fascination with Rome. The Eternal City forms the backdrop to many of his best-loved movies, including *The Nights of Cabiria, La dolce vita* and *Fellini's Satyricon.* The idea of a feature-length documentary about the city predates *The Clowns.* Fellini expressed an interest in depicting "a Rome anthropomorphised, seen like a woman whom one loves and hates at the same time; or like a universe which one believes one knows well because it has always been there, and which, all of a sudden, reveals itself completely unknown, like an unexplored jungle."[16]

With *Roma*, the director headed straight to the heart of the jungle. He employs elements of documentary and autobiography to create a typically Fellinian blend of fiction and fantasy. The film opens with his earliest impressions of Rome, as taught in school and depicted on the stage and screen. Next we see a young man arriving at Termini station. This romanticised Fellini surrogate, who may also remind us of Moraldo, makes his way first to a rooming house and then to a restaurant. Both are unruly and overrun. Rome is exciting and somewhat overwhelming. The various entertainments of the city down the ages are depicted. A wartime variety show is interrupted by an air raid, sending performers and audience underground. (Fellini continues a subterranean exploration of the city with a look at the ongoing construction of a subway system.) The city's brothels are also overcrowded and, in one of them, our young protagonist chooses a heavily made-up brunette whom he misguidedly asks on a date after their business is done. Somewhat daringly, Fellini juxtaposes the whorehouse episode with an ecclesiastical fashion show, consisting of a procession of nuns and priests dressed in increasingly outlandish outfits. Next, Fellini's crew travelled to Trastevere, where a group of intellectuals muse in a street café. In a sinister coda to the film a pack of leather-clad bikers race around the city, the director's mobile camera capturing them en route against the city's ruins.

Roma is a collage tribute to the city, as seen by tourists, locals, a film crew, new arrivals and, of course, Fellini. As such, it is similar to *The Clowns.* The two films share a heartfelt and sentimental tone, aided in *Roma* by the gentle narration of Neapolitan comedian Alghiero Noschese. As in *The Clowns*, Fellini sets himself questions and attempts to answer them with his crew. "What about the Rome of

Still from 'Roma' (1972)
In one of his most savage attacks on religion, Fellini presents the church as a glittering Las Vegas show.

"When the film is quite finished I abandon it with distaste. I have never seen one of my films in a public hall. I am assailed by a kind of prudery, sort of like someone who doesn't want to see a friend do things which he wouldn't do."

Federico Fellini

ABOVE
Still from 'Roma' (1972)
The rebellion of youth is shown through street
demonstrations, hippies and leatherclad bikers.
They are the new barbarians overrunning the
Eternal City.

RIGHT
Still from 'Roma' (1972)
Liberated women bathing in modern Rome.

Still from 'Roma' (1972)
As well as criticising hypocrisy in modern Rome, Fellini gives us a guided tour of the magnificent city.

LEFT
Still from 'Roma' (1972)
A rich woman bathing in ancient Rome. Fellini juxtaposes ancient and modern incidents to comment on them.

today?" he asks. "What impression does it make on the visitor arriving for the first time?" His query is swiftly answered by footage of a traffic pile-up reminiscent of Godard's apocalyptic *Week-End* (1967).

The film is another intriguing mixture of the real and the artificial. While key sights, such as the Spanish Steps and the Trevi Fountain, are faithfully depicted in documentary-style footage, sections of the film were shot at Cinecittà. A strip of road half a kilometre long was laboriously recreated by Danilo Donati. Other interiors, including a vaudeville theatre and a mansion, were also built for the film. Such follies helped push up an already hefty budget.

Fellini arranged a number of cameos for his intimate study of the city. While the appearances of Mastroianni and Sordi ended up on the cutting room floor, two important encounters remain. Before the closing biker scene, Fellini meets Anna Magnani. The encounter marks the final onscreen appearance of an actress he introduces as a symbol of the city itself. Novelist Gore Vidal also appears, enthusiastically explaining why he chooses to live in the Eternal City. "Rome," Vidal believes, "is the city of illusions." With *Roma*, the *maestro* delivers an imaginary journey that is hard to forget.

ABOVE
On the set of 'Roma' (1972)
Fellini in his trademark hat and scarf.

RIGHT
Still from 'Roma' (1972)
Gladiatorial combat in ancient Rome.

ABOVE
On the set of 'Roma' (1972)
The family eating together is an important part of Italian life.

LEFT
Still from 'Roma' (1972)
A student protest is broken up by the Roman police.

PAGES 138/139
On the set of 'Roma' (1972)
As in 'La dolce vita' Fellini recreates the streets of Rome inside the walls of Cinecittà film studios.

"I consider Rome my private apartment. That is the seduction secret of Rome. It's not like being in a city, it is like being in an apartment. The streets are like corridors. Rome is still the mother. Rome is protective."

Federico Fellini[23]

RIGHT
Still from 'Roma' (1972)
Fellini mixes anecdote with interviews and lyrical sequences. The film is peppered with all types of performers.

BELOW
Still from 'Roma' (1972)
Fellini shows different jobs as performances. The women in the 1930s brothel display their wares to prospective clients like models on a catwalk.

OPPOSITE
Still from 'Roma' (1972)
The Pope makes his entrance with all the glamour and glitter of a rock star.

ABOVE
Still from 'Amarcord' (1973)
Titta (Bruno Zanin, left) is a Fellini substitute.
Here he touches the knee of Gradisca (Magali
Noël) in the cinema.

OPPOSITE TOP
Still from 'Amarcord' (1973)
The storyteller Biscein claims to have slept with
every one of the thirty wives of the emir when
they stayed at the Grand Hotel.

OPPOSITE BOTTOM
Still from 'Amarcord' (1973)
The tobacconist (Maria Antonietta Beluzzi)
displays her charms to Titta.

*"… you can see from [Amarcord] that I learned
little in school. To compensate, I enjoyed myself
a lot. More than Greek, Latin, mathematics,
chemistry, none of which I remember any more –
not a verse, a phrase, a digit, a formula – I learned
to develop a spirit of observation."*

Federico Fellini [22]

With this love letter to his adopted city finished, Fellini turned his attentions to
the town of his youth. Both *The Clowns* and *Roma* featured scenes based on
his childhood – indications that as he entered his fifties Fellini's thoughts were
increasingly with Rimini. In 1972 the Christmas edition of *Vogue* carried a number of pieces written by Fellini based on his memories of his provincial youth.
His follow-up to *Roma*, the fanciful and offbeat *Amarcord*, was born out of a
series of caricatures based on people he knew as a child. The film, co-written
with Tonino Guerra, was shot from January to June 1972.

  Amarcord is a year-in-the-life portrait of a resort town named Borgo, clearly
modelled on Rimini. Opening and closing with the arrival of the 'puffballs' that
signal the end of winter and the start of spring, the film follows the exploits of
the mischievous 15-year-old Titta (Bruno Zanin). In 1930s Borgo, as in Rimini,
spring brings hordes of tourists who come to stay at the glamorous Grand
Hotel. Titta spends his time causing havoc around town with his friends, incur-
ring the wrath of his cranky and over-worked father. Hounded by Catholicism
and Fascism at every street corner, Titta and his gang escape into a fantasy world,
dreaming of the town's women. This inspires some energetic self-abuse, which
comes back to haunt them at confession. Titta's episodic adventures include an
excursion with his mad uncle, a clinch with local sexpot Gradisca in the cinema,
and the passing of the real-life *Rex* ocean liner. The film ends with two ceremonies marking the end of his adolescence: the funeral of his mother and the
wedding of Gradisca, who leaves Borgo.

  Amarcord is peppered with some of Fellini's finest screen caricatures, including the pompous lawyer who narrates the film and Titta's sex-obsessed
grandfather. Many of the female caricatures have their origins in Fellini's earlier
films. Set against the innocent Aldina is the white-haired town tramp Volpina,
a figure reminiscent of Saraghina. Borgo has its fair share of *vitelloni*, and
the town idiot Guidizio also reappears from Fellini's third film. The children in
Amarcord are obviously destined for the crisis of the *vitelloni*. Both films end

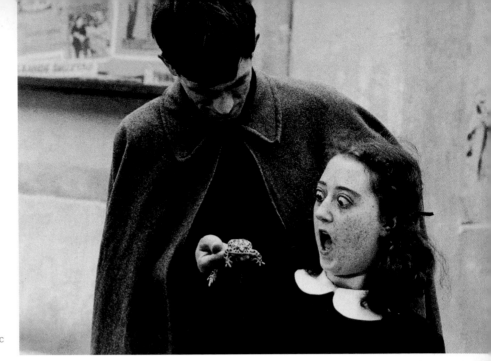

RIGHT
Still from 'Amarcord' (1973)
Children will be children.

BELOW
Still from 'Amarcord' (1973)
Volpina (Josiane Tanzilli) the mad nymphomaniac
wanders the town in a daze.

mc-63

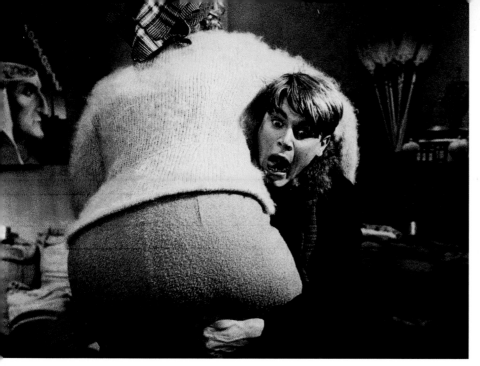

LEFT
Still from 'Amarcord' (1973)
Titta sometimes finds himself holding more than
he can handle. In this case, the tobacconist.

BELOW
Still from 'Amarcord' (1973)
Titta's mother Miranda (Pupella Maggio, middle)
is angry that Titta pissed on Mr Blondi's hat from
the cinema balcony.

Still from 'Amarcord' (1973)
As in 'I vitelloni', this film records important family and community moments. Here Gradisca celebrates her marriage to police officer Matteo.

with the symbolic departure of one of the central characters. Fellini is unable to present such an enclosed world without offering the possibility of escape for those who persevere. The film's closing line ("Titta went away some time ago") suggests not only Titta's eventual departure but also Fellini's own escape from Rimini.

Titta was based on Fellini's close childhood friend Luigi Benzi. In a scene recalling Fausto's attempts to seduce a stranger in *I vitelloni*, Titta tentatively tries his luck with Gradisca during a screening of William Wellman's *Beau Geste* (1939). Fellini claimed the episode was based on his own childhood, but it actually belonged to Benzi. (The same experience had also provided the basis for one of Fellini's contributions to *Marc'Aurelio*.) Many of the colourful scenes in *Amarcord* recall Fellini's own youth. He played similar pranks at school, spied on the banquets and balls held at the Grand Hotel and eagerly awaited the exit from church of the town's fat-bottomed women.

Fellini chose to recreate Rimini rather than return to the provinces. Due to extensive post-war reconstruction, the coastal town had changed significantly since his childhood. The Fulgor was rebuilt at Cinecittà and the front gates of the studios doubled as a railway entrance. A substitute for the Grand Hotel was found in Anzio. One of designer Danilo Donati's most difficult endeavours on the film was the creation of Mussolini's *Rex* ocean liner. He used a model, set against sheets of polythene, to create the effect of its journey.

The humour in *Amarcord* is of a juvenile nature, the gags usually revolving around bodily functions. Belching, farting, urinating and masturbating are the boys' principal sources of amusement. Such toilet humour is combined with the satirical presentation of religion and Fascism. Titta ridicules the priests yet he remains scared of them. Mussolini is equally feared. In a fantasy wedding sequence we are faced with the demonic glare of Il Duce. Titta's father is rudely awakened in the middle of the night by a group of Fascists who consider him a potential anarchist, and he is taken to their offices and forced to drink castor oil. *Amarcord* was Fellini's last commercially successful film. It was selected as the opening film at Cannes in 1973 and won the director another Oscar for Best Foreign Film. As the decade progressed, Fellini fell out of favour with the critics. Having seemingly exorcised his childhood memories once and for all with *Amarcord*, he turned his attentions to one of Italy's famed historical figures – Casanova, the original 'Latin lover' of the Enlightenment.

ABOVE
Still from 'Amarcord' (1973)
The Fascists are ridiculed by Fellini. As a boy Fellini was part of the Fascist youth movement, and in 1937 a Fascist magazine paid him to draw caricatures of boys he went camping with.

PAGES 148/149
Still from 'Amarcord' (1973)
The whole town goes out in boats to wave to the 'Rex' ocean liner returning from America.

Thanks to the 1960 publication of his 12-volume autobiography *L'Histoire de ma vie jusqu'à l'an 1797*, Casanova had received something of an image makeover. He emerged not only as a sex-obsessed hedonist, but also as an intellectual of artistic temperament, not to mention something of a *bidonista*. Fellini researched the project by examining Casanova's *Memoirs* with his co-writer Zapponi. The director quickly became bored. As in *Fellini's Satyricon* and *Roma*, he decided to film his own version of the subject matter. *Fellini's Casanova* went into production and with a budget of $10 million it was his most expensive film yet.

In the lead role Fellini cast Donald Sutherland, whose astonishingly realistic sex scenes with Julie Christie in *Don't Look Now* (1973) had caused considerable public attention. (Fellini had met the Canadian actor briefly in 1970, on the set of Paul Mazursky's *Alex in Wonderland*, in which Sutherland plays a film-maker who tracks down Fellini to ask him some advice.) Fellini's choice proved controversial and was ridiculed by some. Surely Mastroianni, with his legendary reputation and charismatic public persona, would have been a more suitable option? Fellini stood by Sutherland, memorably describing him to Costanzo Costantini as "a big sperm-full waxwork with the eyes of a masturbator."[17] Sutherland was much in awe of his Italian director and arrived on set having thoroughly researched the role. Fellini told him to forget everything. The shoot proved gruelling. Sutherland was required to spend hours in make-up each day – his hair was partially shaved, his eyebrows plucked and his facial features exaggerated. He was required for almost every scene in the film.

For Fellini, Casanova was a *stronzo* – a turd. In his film the prolific lover is a dissipated, melancholic, mechanical man. (Fellini likened him to a puppet, a Pinocchio who never grew up.) The film opens in Venice, with a typically Fellinian carnival, during which a statue of Venus is half raised out of the canals. The statue, with its bulbous blue eyes, is as potent an opening motif as the figure of Christ in *La dolce vita*. Venice is a mass of lanterns, masks and fireworks. As the crowds disperse, Casanova meets and copulates monotonously with a nun. Their performance is watched by Casanova's mechanical bird (flapping its wings like a perambulator as its owner pumps away) and a voyeuristic French ambassador.

Following this interlude Casanova is incarcerated for, amongst other things, the practice of black magic. He escapes to Paris and travels around Europe. Moving from city to city he enjoys a number of sexual encounters. The women he favours vary in size, character and nationality. Annamaria is a sickly young girl he seemingly 'cures' in bed. Madame d'Urfé believes that if Casanova impregnates her she will find immortality. He falls for the beautiful Henrietta in Parma, but she leaves him in the middle of the night. The rejection leads him to consider suicide. His spirits are raised in Rome as he competes with a coachman to see who can perform the sexual act the most times in the space of an hour. In Switzerland his taste for new sensations is sated by an evening with a hunchbacked actress. In Dresden he has a fleeting encounter with his mother. Wearying of his travels, he is delighted to find a life-size mechanical doll, which he takes to bed, recognising his own reflection in the soulless automaton. Mechanical man and mechanical women are briefly united. Casanova ends his days as a Count's librarian, where he is mocked by the servants, who plaster one of his self-portraits onto the toilet wall with excrement. He remains at the end of his life, for the servants and for Fellini, a *stronzo*.

Still from 'Fellini's Casanova' (1976)
Casanova (Donald Sutherland) and Annamaria (Clarissa Roll), the anaemic embroiderer, whom he cured of a life of bloodletting after a night of lovemaking.

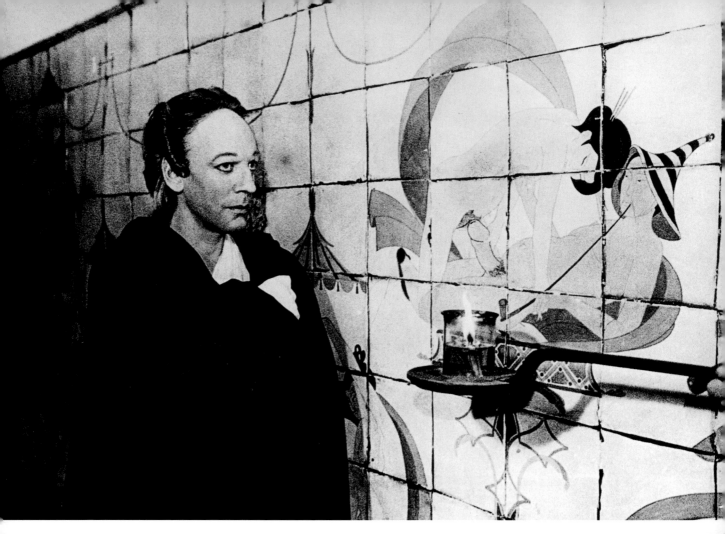

ABOVE
Still from 'Fellini's Casanova' (1976)
Sister Maddalena shows Casanova what is
required from him.

RIGHT
Still from 'Fellini's Casanova' (1976)
The sexual act becomes repetitive for Casanova
but still he is compelled to continue it *ad
infinitum*. Here he warms up in preparation for
the lovemaking contest.

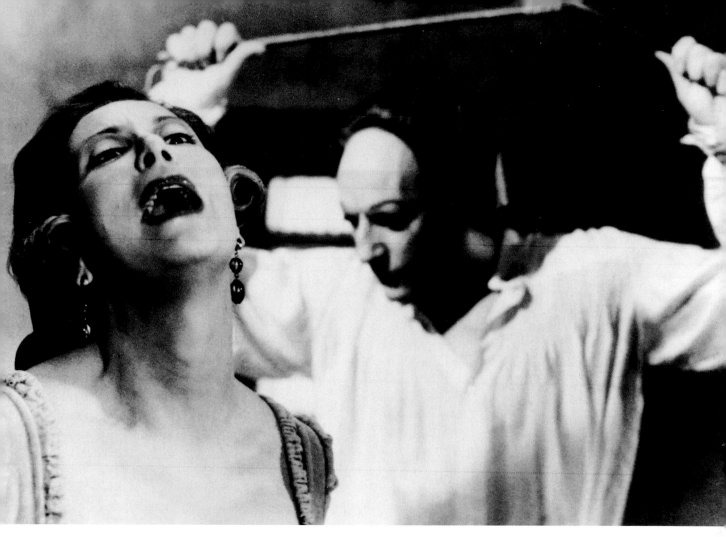

ABOVE
Still from 'Fellini's Casanova' (1976)
Women of all types are attracted to Casanova and he is unable to say no. Here he whips Giselda (Daniela Gatti).

LEFT
Still from 'Fellini's Casanova' (1976)
Sister Maddalena's (Margaret Clementi) prayers are answered.

PAGES 154/155
Still from 'Fellini's Casanova' (1976)
Casanova is held aloft after winning a contest to find out who could make love the most times in an hour.

Fellini likened his *Casanova* to *La dolce vita*. It exposes a similar world of joyless vice. Like Marcello, Casanova wanders from one orgy to the next, from one bed to another. Also, like *La dolce vita* and the equally foggy *Fellini's Satyricon*, it is totally overblown in every department, using 54 sets and a cast of 600. Like *Fellini's Satyricon*, it contains the best and the worst of Fellini. The principal flaw is with the central character. As Casanova's *Memoirs* had proved, the Latin lover was also a man of letters, a mathematician and a politician whose interests included economics, the sciences and the occult. Like the French ambassador who watches him screw, yet exits before hearing him talk, Fellini refuses this much-maligned historical figure a chance to defend himself.

Fellini's Casanova was a commercial failure everywhere in the world except Japan. Critical reaction to the film was mixed. The heartfelt *Amarcord* had been warmly welcomed with opened arms. This detached and emotionally empty study got a cold reception from many. Some berated Fellini for what they saw as his objectification of the female form, as opposed to Casanova's. That the film proved Fellini's skill as a director was undeniable. Certainly there is much to celebrate in *Fellini's Casanova*. Rota delivered another complex score, featuring an atmospheric music box motif to accompany the protagonist's mechanical bird. Sutherland gives an astonishing central performance and the recreation of Venice is staggering. (Danilo Donati's costume design was recognised with a plethora of awards.) Nevertheless, Vincent Canby's review for *The New York Times* summed up popular opinion: 'Federico Fellini has created another revel of a movie – spectacular but singularly joyless.'[18] Where was the enjoyment in watching the repetitive sex life of a soulless protagonist?

Still from 'Fellini's Casanova' (1976)
Unable to get excited by women, Casanova finds himself in love with a machine, Rosalba (Adele Angela Lojodice), which is a reflection of himself.

Fellini's established pattern of following up excessive fantasy productions with smaller, more measured pictures continued after *Fellini's Casanova*. *Orchestra Rehearsal*, a short parable about an anarchic orchestra, was shot in just 16 days using one set. The film was inspired by the high-profile kidnapping of politician and former Prime Minister Aldo Moro, who was first abducted and then murdered by Red Brigade terrorists in 1978. *Orchestra Rehearsal* is set in an ancient church oratory in which the members of an orchestra gradually assemble to rehearse a symphony. As they take their places some listen to a football match on the radio, others look at smutty magazines and a couple even discuss the psychoanalytic qualities of *8 1/2*. A television crew records the action for a documentary. Before long, squabbles break out among the members of the orchestra about the worth of their respective instruments. Each musician has an inflated sense of his own importance. The dictatorial tone of the over-theatrical conductor ("I should castrate you all!") angers the players, who become argumentative. Finally, they unite against him. As the drums sound out a tribal beat, slogans are chanted and sprayed on the wall, a couple make love under a piano and fights break out between the various sections of the orchestra. Rebelling against their conductor and the music they are forced to play, the musicians run riot until the walls crack from the force of a hammer and the rehearsal resumes.

    Orchestra Rehearsal is the least Fellinian of the director's movies in the 1970s, if not his whole career. With its stark contemporary setting, short running time and modest budget it is the antithesis of *Fellini's Casanova*. It is no less ambitious, however, and the result is equally powerful. As an ironic and detached allegory or essay about the evils of totalitarianism it marks the first political statement from Fellini, who had hitherto refused to discuss that aspect of his work. With reference to Spengler's *The Decline of the West*, the film is subtitled *The Decline of the West in C# Major*. *Orchestra Rehearsal* is an astonishingly objective work from a film-maker who had become increasingly subjective. Similarities to earlier films abound. Fellini's love of caricature, so pronounced in *Amarcord*, returns here. Many of the members of the orchestra were real musicians chosen by the director. Like *Amarcord*, the film is narrated by an amicable, bumbling character. Like *8 1/2*, *Orchestra Rehearsal* is set against a backdrop of the arts and reveals a work-in-progress – not only the orchestra's symphony but also the TV crew's documentary. Fellini also can't stop himself aligning his role as a director to that of a conductor. (The conductor in the film is referred to as *maestro*.)

    Unlike much of Fellini's later work, *Orchestra Rehearsal* has stood the test of time well. As a reflection on how we can live in times of chaos it achieves a whole new currency in the wake of continuing terrorist activity around the world. The film was first screened to an audience of politicians at the Quirinale, where it received a frosty reception. Although originally made for the TV network RAI, it received a theatrical release and proved a domestic success. It was dedicated to Nino Rota, who died shortly after completing work on the film's score. The taut political essay seemed to herald a new direction for the film-maker. However, any assumptions that Fellini had changed directions in his old age were erased by his next picture.

On the set of 'Orchestra Rehearsal' (1979)
Fellini conducts the action.

"I am not an orator, a philosopher or a theorist. I am merely a story-teller and the cinema is my work."

ABOVE
Still from 'Orchestra Rehearsal' (1979)
In this political allegory the orchestra eventually revolts against the conductor.

LEFT
On the set of 'Orchestra Rehearsal' (1979)
Fellini often played a musical instrument on the set, whether it be a xylophone, a trombone or, in this case, a trumpet.

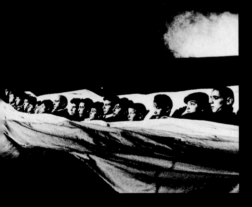

City of Women marks the return of some all-too-familiar Fellini motifs. Opening
with another train journey, the film re-investigates sex, voyeurism, fantasy and
the dream world. Once more, Mastroianni appears as the alter egoist. ("With
Marcello again? Maestro, please," a female voice giggles as the opening credits
appear.)

The idea for *City of Women* originated in an evening Fellini spent with Ingmar
Bergman, during which the film-makers decided to collaborate on a two-part film
with a common theme. Bergman conceived the story of an affair, while Fellini
and his co-writer Zapponi sketched a tale about a womaniser confronted by a
group of angry feminists. The collaboration between the directors, to be called
Love Duet, never happened. Nevertheless, each tale grew into a full-length feature. Bergman's became his first English-language feature, *The Touch*, released
in 1970. Fellini's *City of Women* took a decade longer to reach the screen. It was
influenced on the way by Fellini's friendship with popular Belgian novelist
Georges Simenon who, as a member of the jury at Cannes, had secured *La dolce
vita*'s resounding success. Simenon, who claimed to have bedded 10,000 women,
was a model for Dr Katzone, one of the film's central characters.

As usual, Fellini found it hard to find a producer. The first, *Penthouse* publisher
Bob Guccione, withdrew when the director went over-budget. He was replaced
by Daniel Toscan du Plantier. Production difficulties began with Nino Rota's
death and continued during the shoot itself. Ettore Manni, the actor who plays
Katzone, died after six weeks of filming and the shoot was suspended as the
scriptwriters reworked the storyline. Mastroianni suffered from an infected sty,
for which he required a number of operations, while Fellini took a week out with
a broken arm. That *City of Women* eventually reached completion (the shoot
ended eight months after it began) was something of a minor miracle.

The film opens on a train. Our hero, Snàporaz, enjoys a brief clinch with a
mysterious woman. As the train reaches her stop she alights. Snàporaz follows
her into a forest and loses sight of her. Searching through the forest he comes
across a hotel hosting a convention. Hordes of aggressive women line the walls,

angrily debating burning issues like marriage, masturbation, intercourse and fellatio. He spots the woman from the train but she ridicules him in front of the crowd. He escapes from the convention, only to be picked up first by a woman who attempts to rape him, and then by a group of dangerous rebels. Snàporaz seeks refuge at the house of Dr Katzoné, an ageing lothario about to celebrate his 10,000th sexual conquest. In one of the film's most distinctive and successful sequences, he passes through Katzone's gallery of former lovers, listening to audio samples of their sexual encounters. He also views a strange procession of women from his childhood who have formed the basis of his erotic fantasies. Snàporaz's stay is interrupted by the arrival of a group of angry feminists who bring him to trial. He escapes, clinging to a huge floating hot air balloon shaped like a woman. As he ascends, a lone sniper below opens fire on the balloon and he is left dangling helplessly in mid-air. Cut to the train from the opening scene: Snàporaz awakens abruptly, sat opposite his wife. "What's eating you?" she asks, as he looks around in confusion. "You've been mumbling and moaning for two hours."

The extent of Snàporaz's real-life success with women is never fully revealed but it is clear he strives to be a modern day Casanova. *City of Women* recalls Fellini's equally ambitious biopic, which also suffered from an excessive running time, an unwieldy cast and an overblown budget. The germ for the film can be found in *8 1/2*'s harem sequence, in which the women revolt against their master, Guido. One of Guido's acquaintances in the film refers to him affectionately as Snàporaz. In real life, Fellini had long used the same nickname for his friend Mastroianni. Snàporaz, like Guido, tries to understand himself through an analysis of the women in his life. Just as the film echoes the themes of earlier films, it repeats exact sequences. For example, one scene sees a row of young boys in bed, masturbating over images of Mae West on a huge cinema screen. (Fellini had repeatedly tried to cast her in his films.) *Amarcord* had featured a scene in which a group of boys masturbate collectively in a small car, calling out the names of desirable women.

ABOVE
Still from 'City of Women' (1980)
Snàporaz enjoys the hallway of his friend Sante
Katzone, which contains images and sounds of
Katzone's ten thousand sexual encounters.

RIGHT
Still from 'City of Women' (1980)
Snàporaz performs a song and dance routine
with Sara (Rosaria Tafuri) and Donatella
(Donatella Damiani) at Katzone's party.

Fellini described *City of Women* as almost entirely a dream. By interweaving his character's fantasies into a dreamlike structure the film recalls *Juliet of the Spirits*, another attempt to enter the female psyche. The film was met with accusations of anti-feminism. Critics ridiculed its all too obvious Freudian symbolism (Katzone kisses and caresses a statue of his mother, Snàporaz's train enters an Hitchcockian tunnel in the opening and closing scenes). Althought Fellini had been a director for 30 years, audiences still questioned how well he understood women. In a sense Fellini safeguards himself in *City of Women* by using the comedy genre and a dream structure. The film can be considered as simply a comedy or fantasy rather then as a serious examination of the modern woman and contemporary sexual relationships. But, unfortunately, it's a failure on either count. *Amarcord*'s schoolboy humour suited the subject matter, Snàporaz's repellent and juvenile objectification of women is, well, repellent. Both turgid and tedious, the film is an exaggeration of everything that is infuriating about Fellini's later work. The *maestro* had begun to repeat himself.

On the set of 'City of Women' (1980)
The production was plagued by deaths, births, marriages, accidents, illnesses, explosions, strikes and so on. Fellini even broke his arm.

The Circus Leaves Town 1983–1993

With *8 1/2*, *Fellini: A Director's Notebook*, *The Clowns* and *Roma*, Fellini examined the film industry from a number of different angles. In the 1980s, he turned his attentions first to grand opera (*And the Ship Sails On*), then to television (*Ginger and Fred*) and finally to the cinema with *Intervista*.

In the nostalgic *And the Ship Sails On*, the ashes of a famous opera singer are taken out to sea by the *Gloria N.* to be dispersed around the island of Erimo. Onboard are a horde of guests, including a Prussian Grand Duke and a host of opera singers. Fellini methodically follows the ritual, performed in the summer of 1914, using a relatively simplistic narrative structure. Like *Orchestra Rehearsal* the film has a first-person narrator, Orlando (Freddie Jones), who introduces himself in the opening scenes. (Umberto Zuanelli, the copyist who narrates the earlier film, reappears in *And the Ship Sails On* in a minor role.) We watch the little intrigues onboard unfold until, on the third day, a party of shipwrecked Serbians appear. At first fearful and suspicious of the new arrivals, the majority of the guests keep them out of sight. However, when the Serbians put on a dance, the others recognise their humanity. When an Austro-Hungarian fleet arrives, demanding the Serbians' return, they are cast out in a lifeboat and an accidental prank performed by one of the Serbians leads to the capsizing of the *Gloria N.* Orlando escapes and sails off bemused.

Fellini's choice of opera as the artistic background for this film is unusual. Despite his country's rich operatic tradition, and the celebrated work in that field carried out by Nino Rota, his closest collaborator, Fellini had never professed an interest in the art form. (Although he had, of course, chosen to film an orchestra for the central metaphor in *Orchestra Rehearsal*.) Despite this operatic background, the film works as a tribute to cinema's rich history. The opening minutes form a brief reminder of the art form's progression over the century. The film opens like a flickering, black and white silent movie, complete with title cards lettered in an old-fashioned font. (Fellini commented that he "wanted the characters of the story to convey the same feeling as when you look at an old photograph."[19]) The action, which is sped up as in the first silent comedies, is accompanied by the sound of a projector. The film bleeds into sepia tones, and then colour. As it does so, sound effects are replaced with musical accompani-

Still from 'And the Ship Sails On' (1983)
The lovesick rhinoceros is loaded onto the 'Gloria N.'

"I love Cinecittà. I've spent the happiest part of my working life there. It's my factory, it's where I work and it's a good working tool."

Federico Fellini[21]

Still from 'And the Ship Sails On' (1983)
Journalist Orlando (Freddie Jones) talks to
innocent Dorotea (Sara Jane Varley) in an attempt
to extract gossip about the celebrities on the ship,
rather like Marcello in 'La dolce vita.'

ment. *And the Ship Sails On* looks and feels a bit more like a modern movie
until the final reel, when it follows the same pattern in reverse, leaving a sense
of nostalgia.

Like Fellini's major productions in the previous decade, *And the Ship Sails
On* was made on a grand scale. During the film's 16-week shoot, Fellini used
over 100 actors (many of them British) and ten of Cinecittà's stages. Studio 5
encompassed the entire ship's deck, while its exterior was painted on the wall of
a Roman pasta factory. Like some of the set designs for his earlier work, the film
makes a show of its artificiality throughout. ("It looks painted," comments one
woman, staring at an artificial sunset.) As the narrative unfolds, Fellini – ever the
playful magician – takes delight in showing the audience the behind-the-scenes
processes involved in making the movie. At the end of the film, Dante Ferretti's
false sea is exposed, like Donati's studio-built ocean in *Amarcord*, revealing a
mass of black plastic sheets and glitter.

And the Ship Sails On is Fellini's third period piece, after *Fellini's Satyricon* and
Fellini's Casanova, and his first film to be set outside Italy. It uses two familiar
Fellinian tropes: the journey and the sea. As we have seen, the sea forms a sym-
bolic and predominantly melancholic landscape in many of the *maestro*'s films.
His interest in the journey is akin to his fascination with the 'work-in-progress' –
which is also suggested in this film by the journalistic research conducted by
Orlando. One of Fellini's many journalist characters, Orlando interviews various
guests in a manner reminiscent of the reporters in Fellini's pseudo-documentaries.
The type of people he questions – chiefly aristocrats and celebrities – are not dis-

similar to those chased along the via Veneto by that other reporter, Marcello Rubini, in *La dolce vita*.

And the Ship Sails On benefits from a perfectly measured pace and a light tone, helped by the gentle narration from the amiable Orlando. It is frequently very amusing and relies on comedy of character. Like *Orchestra Rehearsal* the individuals within the group are distinctively drawn – Fellini's talent for caricature is still evident. The film paints a kaleidoscopic group portrait, from the high society on deck to the workers below, making the ship – like Fellini's film sets and circuses – a microcosm of society. A remarkably youthful film for a director nearing the age of 70, *And the Ship Sails On* contains several imaginative touches. The musical interludes, often misplaced in earlier films, are successfully integrated with the narrative. One of Fellini's most accessible movies, it was screened out of competition at Venice and was more successful than the excessive *City of Women*.

ABOVE
Still from 'And the Ship Sails On' (1983)
The Austro-Hungarian battleship steams into range of the 'Gloria N.' to collect the Serbians who had boarded the previous night.

LEFT
Still from 'And the Ship Sails On' (1983)
The ashes of the great opera singer Edmea Tetuo are scattered off the island of Erimo.

PAGES 168/169
Still from 'And the Ship Sails On' (1983)
Orlando helps the rhinoceros escape from the sinking 'Gloria N.'

Still from 'Ginger and Fred' (1985)
Aurelio (Franco Fabrizi) introduces the absurd television show.

"Television is destroying everything."

Federico Fellini [20]

For his next feature Fellini again used a traditional narrative structure. *Ginger and Fred* was originally conceived for a TV series featuring episodes from different film-makers, including Antonioni and Franco Zeffirelli. Like so many similar projects, this fell through. However, Fellini persevered with his episode, garnering multinational funding and turning it into a full-length feature. The film was written for Masina and marks the only time that Masina and Marcello Mastroianni played opposite each other for Fellini. Appropriately, the storyline revolves around a reunion. (Masina and Fellini hadn't worked together since 1965's *Juliet of the Spirits*.) Also reunited with the director is Franco Fabrizi, the star of *I vitelloni* and *Il bidone*.

Ginger (Masina) and Fred (Mastroianni) are old flames and former variety show dancers. They achieved a certain success in the 1940s when they mimicked the steps of their more famous namesakes, Rogers and Astaire. They are reunited in the 1980s when they are invited to perform on a popular TV show. Like so many Fellinian protagonists before her, Ginger arrives at a railway station in the opening reel. On the way to her hotel she witnesses the cultural domination of television. A TV salesman loiters around the station, a personal TV set

ABOVE
Still from 'Ginger and Fred' (1985)
Passive widow Amelia Bonetti (Giulietta Masina)
and impish Pippo Botticella (Marcello
Mastroianni) meet for the first time in forty
years to relive their years as Ginger and Fred.

LEFT
On the set of 'Ginger and Fred' (1985)
The purpose of television is to sell products
using sex and violence. It is unfortunate that
sometimes programmes are inserted between
the adverts.

Still from 'Ginger and Fred' (1985)
The ageing dance couple reform for a TV show
and find themselves not only relics but objects of
ridicule.

plays in the bus that takes her to the hotel and the hotel staff are preoccupied
with a televised football game. Ginger admits that her grandchildren are TV
junkies.

    At the hotel, she finds an unruly collection of misfits and artists who are also
appearing on the show and would seem more at home in a circus. Tired and dis-
tressed, she goes to bed but is kept awake by some loud snoring from the room
next door. When she goes to complain she finds that the snorer is a drunken and
dishevelled Fred. The couple are reunited. On the day of the show both are nerv-
ous. The superstitious Fred clutches a horseshoe, damning those around him as
amateurs. The other guests include a woman who has left her family for an extra-
terrestrial, a dangerous Mafioso and a troupe of midget musicians. The hoofers
have only a brief half hour to rehearse and soon find themselves onstage. Despite
a false start due to an electrical fault, and a momentary slip by Fred during a tap
dance, the magic is still there. Their performance is one of the most touching
sequences in the *maestro*'s oeuvre.

    As in *And the Ship Sails On*, Fellini combines this film's gentle narrative with
some ferocious social satire. This time, television comes under attack. The variety
show programme is laden with commercials that interrupt the flow of the routines and the kind of inane gossip seen on today's chat shows. Indeed, many
of the guests, such as the transvestite who frequents Italian jails, wouldn't seem
out of place on *The Jerry Springer Show*. While focusing primarily on television,

Fellini's film also becomes a melancholy swansong for the Hollywood of yester-year, just as *And the Ship Sails On* reflects on the history of cinema.

Fellini looks once more at the magnetic power of celebrity in this film. The show features a host of lookalikes including lookalikes of Bette Davis, Woody Allen and Clark Gable. Fellini's films have always depicted characters obsessed with the famous, from Wanda (infatuated with the White Sheik) to Cabiria (in awe of handsome movie star Alberto Lazarri). Here, his characters lose their own identity by aping the behaviour of those in the spotlight. Ginger and Fred's act is a tribute to other performers, relying on public awareness of Rogers and Astaire for its success. Ginger Rogers herself found the film offensive and sued. As affectionate, nostalgic and amusing as *And the Ship Sails On*, the film was mostly well received. It benefits from a charming lilting score, reminiscent of Rota, and has strong central performances.

Still from 'Ginger and Fred' (1985)
Fred shows the audience what he thinks of them.

In 1987, Cinecittà turned 50 and the *maestro* decided to direct a tribute to his personal dream factory. *Intervista*, dismissed by the director as a "filmetto," uses the same mockumentary format as *Roma* and *The Clowns*, and is particularly reminiscent of *Fellini: A Director's Notebook*. Instead of taking the role of the inquisitive reporter himself, Fellini based his film around a Japanese TV crew supposedly making a documentary at Cinecittà. He subsequently becomes the subject of the film. In the atmospheric opening, the TV crew arrive at Cinecittà to follow Fellini's work on an adaptation of Kafka's *Amerika*. This main narrative strand is followed throughout *Intervista*, yet the film is also an examination of Cinecittà itself and of the studios' past. (The crew search for relics from *Quo Vadis?*, *Ben-Hur* and *Cleopatra*.) *Intervista* is also a film about Fellini's childhood. There is a typically romanticised recreation of his first trip to the studios in 1940 to interview a glamorous actress. As such, the film and its title reveal a number of layers. The Japanese crew interview Fellini, as a youth he interviews the actress, and in the film *Intervista* he is really interviewing himself.

As in the earlier pseudo-documentaries, there are some notable cameos in the film. At Cinecittà, Fellini once more meets Mastroianni who, decked out in top hat and tails as Mandrake the Magician, is starring in a commercial. Their reunion inspires them to drive out to Anita Ekberg's house, accompanied by the young actor who plays Fellini in the film's recreation. In a powerfully nostalgic scene set at Ekberg's suburban home, Marcello conjures up a clip from *La dolce vita*. Fellini's mischievous penultimate feature works as a testament to his cinematic vision – a tribute to himself as well as Cinecittà. It also offers far more detailed information about the world behind the scenes on a film set than *8 1/2*. Despite being awarded the Special Jury prize at Cannes, it wasn't screened in the United States or the United Kingdom until five years after its domestic release. While the film is often touching and its valedictory tone reminiscent of *Ginger and Fred*, it is not without its longueurs. Fellini was obviously pleased with it. Asked by *Sight and Sound* magazine to compile a top ten list of his favourite films, he listed it alongside works by Charles Chaplin (*City Lights*, 1931), John Ford (*Stagecoach*, 1939) and Stanley Kubrick (*2001: A Space Odyssey*, 1968). He was the only director polled to include one of his own films. He had also contributed to another of the features on his list, Rossellini's *Paisà*. Until the end the *maestro* was always his own best publicity machine.

"I realised that the cinema offered this miraculous double feature: you tell a story and while you are doing so you are living another one yourself, an adventurous one with people as extraordinary as those in the film you are making. ... like people in the circus who live where they perform as well as on the trains in which they travel."

Federico Fellini [22]

ABOVE
Still from 'Intervista' (1987)
In a film rife with recreations of old memories,
it is fitting that Fellini features an elephant.

LEFT
Still from 'Intervista' (1987)
At every opportunity, Fellini lets us see and hear
the behaviour and attitudes of the people behind
the scenes.

PAGE 176
Still from 'Intervista' (1987)
This pseudo-documentary followed Fellini around
his beloved Cinecittà film studios as he recreated
real and imagined scenes from his past.

PAGE 177
Still from 'Intervista' (1987)
Anita Ekberg is amused when Marcello
Mastroianni, dressed as comic strip hero
Mandrake the Magician, feigns a heart attack.

His next film, *The Voice of the Moon*, would be his last. The provincial comedy
was shot not at Cinecittà but at Dinocittà – the studio complex on via Pontina,
named after the producer Dino De Laurentiis. An adaptation of a contemporary
novel, *Il poema dei lunatici* (*The Poem of Lunatics*), the film once more surprised
both fans and critics. Despite his claims that cinema had nothing to do with the
other arts, particularly literature, Fellini turned to a fictional source for the film.
The novel's author, Ermanno Cavazzoni, assisted with the screenplay. In another
contradictory move, the film was almost completely funded by television, despite
the director's increasingly antagonistic comments about the medium.

In the lead, Fellini cast the popular and versatile comic Roberto Benigni, previously seen sharing a jail cell with Tom Waits and John Lurie in Jim Jarmusch's
Down by Law (1986). A Fellini-Benigni collaboration had been a long time coming. The actor had already read for parts in *City of Women*, *Ginger and Fred* and
Intervista. In *The Voice of the Moon* Benigni plays Ivo, a former patient of a men-
tal hospital. Haunted by mysterious voices emanating from a well, Ivo is first seen
drifting through the fields of a small town in the Po delta. Attracted by the noise
surrounding a nearby house he approaches, finding a group of men watching a

middle-aged woman strip. He leaves the men to it and continues on his way, eventually settling at the cemetery, where he is overcome by memories of his childhood. (One distinctive scene, in which his grandmother puts him to bed, recalls Guido's memories in *8 1/2*.) Ivo's romantic nature is key to the narrative. He is something of a dreamer and frequently quotes from the work of melancholic poet Giacomo Leopardi. When the annual Gnocchi Festival arrives, the town is overcome with noise and disruption. The festival marks the arrival of a local TV station, allowing Fellini to criticise television and advertising in the satirical fashion evinced in *Ginger and Fred*. The mania of the town seems symbolic for Ivo who, surrounded once more by the town's misty countryside, muses, "If things were a little quieter, we might understand something."

The Voice of the Moon is a disappointing coda to the work of a master director. It shows Fellini moving away from both the simple structures of *And the Ship Sails On* and *Ginger and Fred*, and the playful subjectivity of *Intervista*. Critics were unconvinced by his new direction. The same catalogue of Fellinian preoccupations is present, but there is a listlessness inherent in their appearance. The usual scenes of voyeurism and introspection are present, accompanied by the typical carnival. The marginal loner Ivo is reminiscent of some of Fellini's earlier characters, his dream life blurring with reality and fantasy along a picaresque adventure. There is also some familiar characterisation, with the TV crews, Japanese tourists, larger-than-life females and assorted oddballs of Ivo's hometown. As unstructured as *City of Women*, this final feature is equally frustrating. The film failed to secure US distribution and remains largely unknown.

Its unenthusiastic reception made Fellini's customary search for financing nigh on impossible. As he turned 70, he returned to working for the medium he so abhorred, directing a TV commercial for Banca di Roma in 1992. In March 1993 came one final trip to the United States, to receive the lifetime achievement Oscar. During a ceremony that saw Clint Eastwood's *Unforgiven* (1992) and Régis Wargnier's *Indochine* (1991) honoured, Fellini's brief speech and kind words to Masina, who sat in the front row, touched the audience in Hollywood and those watching around the world. In June of the same year, he underwent by-pass surgery in Zurich. He went to Rimini to recover from the operation, staying at the epicentre of his youthful fascination with glitz and glamour – the Grand Hotel. Fellini suffered a stroke at the hotel in August. Another followed two months later and he was pronounced dead on 31 October, some 50 years and a day after he married Masina. His body was laid in state at Cinecittà and visitors flocked to pay their respects. He was later buried in his home town of Rimini. As a mark of honour, the director's favourite sound stage, Studio 5, was subsequently renamed the Teatro Federico Fellini.

Federico Fellini: poet and dreamer, magician and showman, puppeteer and storyteller. His work for the cinema spanned an astonishing seven decades, during which time he told tales of small towns and big cities, nobodies and celebrities, sinners and saints. He created much-loved screen icons such as Gelsomina and Cabiria, onscreen alter egos like Marcello Rubini and Guido Anselmi, and re-imagined historical figures like Casanova. He helped make stars of Marcello Mastroianni, Anouk Aimée, Anita Ekberg and Giulietta Masina. All the while he painstakingly created his own myth. A decade after his death the *maestro*'s myth is still intact.

OPPOSITE
On the set of 'The Voice of the Moon' (1990)
Roberto Benigni being manipulated by puppeteer Federico Fellini.

PAGES 182/183
Federico Fellini
Fellini's camera flies over Rome, as in a dream.

Filmography

Luci del varietà

(Variety Lights, Lights of Variety, 1950)
Crew: *Directors* Federico Fellini & Alberto Lattuada, *Writers* Federico Fellini, Alberto Lattuada, Tullio Pinelli & Ennio Flaiano, *Producers* Federico Fellini & Alberto Lattuada (Capitolium Film), *Cinematographer* Otello Martelli, *Editor* Mario Bonotti, *Music* Felice Lattuada, B&W, 100 minutes.
Cast: Peppino De Filippo (Checco Dalmonte), Carlo Del Poggio (Liliana Antonelli), Giulietta Masina (Melina Amour), John Kitzmiller (John), Giulio Cali (Edison Will, fakir), Alberto Lattuada (theatre menial).
Variety Lights is a comedy about a ragged vaudeville outfit led by a lascivious impresario.

Lo sceicco bianco *(The White Sheik, 1952)*

Crew: *Director* Federico Fellini, *Writers* Federico Fellini, Tullio Pinelli, Ennio Flaiano & Michelangelo Antonioni (story idea), *Producer* Luigi Rovere, *Cinematography* Arturo Gallea, *Editor* Rolando Benedetti, *Music* Nino Rota, B&W, 88 minutes.
Cast: Brunella Bovo (Wanda Cavalli), Leopoldo Trieste (Ivan Cavalli), Alberto Sordi (Fernando Rivoli, the White Sheik), Giulietta Masina (Cabiria).
The White Sheik is a satire in which a woman's love for photostrips disrupts her honeymoon.

I vitelloni

(Spivs, The Young and the Passionate, 1953)
Crew: *Director* Federico Fellini, *Writers* Federico Fellini, Tullio Pinelli & Ennio Flaiano, *Producer* Lorenzo Pegoraro (Peg Films-Cité Films), *Cinematography* Otello Martelli, *Editor* Rolando Benedetti, *Music* Nino Rota, B&W, 103 minutes.
Cast: Franco Interlenghi (Moraldo), Franco Fabrizi (Fausto), Alberto Sordi (Alberto), Leopoldo Trieste (Leopoldo), Riccardo Fellini (Riccardo), Eleonora Ruffo (Sandra), Jean Brochard (Fausto's father), Claude Farrell (Alberto's sister), Carlo Romano (Signor Michele).
I vitelloni is a valedictory drama about a bunch of male layabouts stuck in a small town.

Un'agenzia matrimoniale

(A Matrimonial Agency, 1953)
Episode in the compilation film *Amore in città*
(Love in the City, 1953)
Crew: *Director* Federico Fellini, *Writers* Federico Fellini & Tullio Pinelli, *Producers* Cesare Zavattini, Riccardo Ghione & Marco Ferreri, *Cinematography* Gianni di Venanzo, *Editor* Eraldo da Roma, *Music* Mario Nascimbene, B&W, 32 minutes.
Cast: Antonio Cifariello (journalist), Livia Venturini (Rossana).
A Matrimonial Agency is about a reporter whose actions reverberate on a lonely young woman.

La strada *(The Road, 1954)*

Crew: *Director* Federico Fellini, *Writers* Federico Fellini, Tullio Pinelli & Ennio Flaiano, *Producers* Carlo Ponti & Dino De Laurentiis, *Cinematography* Otello Martelli, *Editor* Leo Catozzo, *Music* Nino Rota, B&W, 115 minutes.
Cast: Giulietta Masina (Gelsomina), Anthony Quinn (Zampanò), Richard Basehart (the Fool), Aldo Silvani (circus owner), Marcella Rovere (widow), Livia Venturini (nun).
La strada is a poetic road movie about the relationship between a circus strongman and a wide-eyed naïf.

Il bidone *(The Swindle, The Swindlers, 1955)*

Crew: *Director* Federico Fellini, *Writers* Federico Fellini, Tullio Pinelli & Ennio Flaiano, *Producers* Titanus & SGG, *Cinematography* Otello Martelli, *Editors* Mario Serandrei & Giuseppe Vari, *Music* Nino Rota, B&W, 104 minutes.
Cast: Broderick Crawford (Augusto), Richard Basehart (Picasso), Franco Fabrizi (Roberto), Giulietta Masina (Iris), Lorella De Luca (Patrizia), Giacomo Gabrielli (Vargas), Sue Ellen Blake (Susanna), Alberto De Amicis (Goffredo), Irena Cefaro (Marisa).
Il bidone is a downbeat crime drama about the various forms of deception.

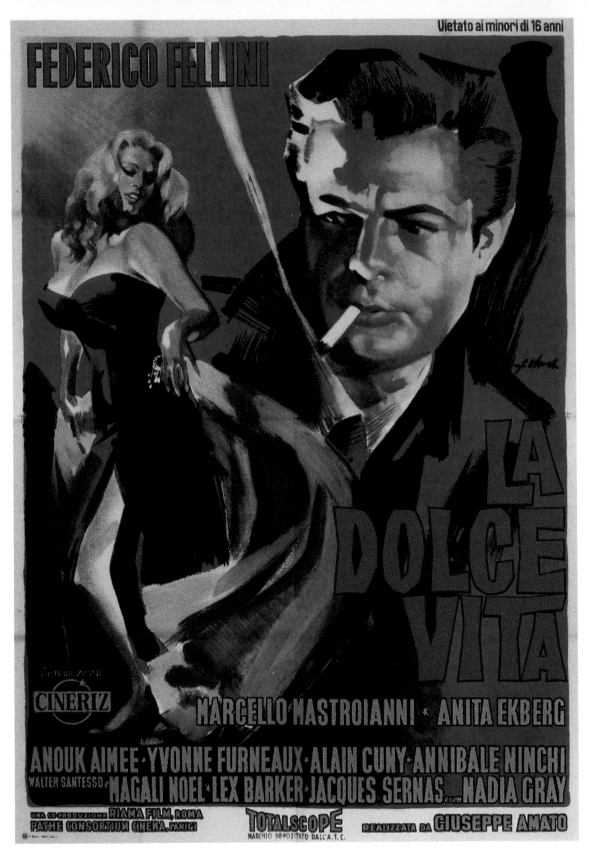

Le notti di Cabiria

(The Nights of Cabiria, 1957)
Crew: *Director* Federico Fellini, *Writers* Federico
Fellini, Tullio Pinelli, Ennio Flaiano & Pier Paolo
Pasolini (dialogue), *Producer* Dino De Laurentiis,
Cinematography Aldo Tonti & Otello Martelli,
Editors Leo Catozzo & Giuseppe Verdi, *Music*
Nino Rota, B&W, 110 minutes.
Cast: Giulietta Masina (Cabiria), Amedeo Nazzari
(the actor), François Périer (Oscar D'Onofrio), Aldo
Silvani (hypnotist), Franca Marzi (Wanda), Dorian
Gray (Jessy), Franco Fabrizi (Giorgio), Mario Passante (the lame man), Pina Gualandri (Matilde).
The Nights of Cabiria is a bittersweet picture about
the trials and tribulations of a long-suffering
Roman prostitute.

La dolce vita *(1960)*

Crew: *Director* Federico Fellini, *Writers* Federico
Fellini, Tullio Pinelli, Ennio Flaiano & Brunello
Rondi, *Producers* Giuseppe Amato & Angelo Rizzoli, *Cinematography* Otello Martelli, *Editor* Leo
Catozzo, *Music* Nino Rota, B&W, 174 minutes.
Cast: Marcello Mastroianni (Marcello Rubini),
Anouk Aimée (Maddalena), Anita Ekberg (Sylvia),
Walter Santesso (Paparazzo), Lex Barker (Robert),
Yvonne Fourneaux (Emma), Alain Cuny (Steiner),
Annibale Ninchi (Marcello's father), Polidor (clown),
Nadia Gray (Nadia), Valeria Ciangottini (Paola).
La dolce vita is a dazzling yet dejected overview of
the bad and the beautiful in 1950s Rome.

Le tentazioni del dottor Antonio

(The Temptations of Doctor Antonio, 1962)
Episode in the compilation film *Boccaccio '70* (1962)
Crew: *Director* Federico Fellini, *Writers* Federico
Fellini, Tullio Pinelli & Ennio Flaiano, *Producers*
Carlo Ponti & Antonio Cervi, *Cinematography*
Otello Martelli, *Editor* Leo Catozzo, *Music* Nino
Rota, B&W, 60 minutes.
Cast: Peppino De Filippo (Doctor Antonio
Mazzuolo), Anita Ekberg (Anita), Donatella
Della Nora (Mazzuolo's sister), Antonio Acqua
(Commendatore La Pappa).
The Temptations of Doctor Antonio is a short satire
on advertising, following an episode in the life of
a hypocritical moral crusader.

Otto e mezzo *(8 1/2, 1963)*

Crew: *Director* Federico Fellini, *Writers* Federico
Fellini, Tullio Pinelli, Ennio Flaiano & Brunello
Rondi, *Producer* Angelo Rizzoli, *Cinematography*
Gianni di Venanzo, *Editor* Leo Catozzo, *Music*
Nino Rota, B&W, 138 minutes.
Cast: Marcello Mastroianni (Guido Anselmi),
Anouk Aimée (Luisa Anselmi), Sandra Milo (Carla),
Claudia Cardinale (Claudia), Rossella Falk
(Rossella), Edra Gale (La Saraghina), Madeleine
Lebeau (the French actress), Barbara Steel (Gloria
Morin).
8 1/2 is an accomplished, autobiographical film
about film-making.

Giulietta degli spiriti

(Juliet of the Spirits, 1965)
Crew: *Director* Federico Fellini, *Writers* Federico
Fellini, Tullio Pinelli, Ennio Flaiano & Brunello
Rondi, *Producer* Angelo Rizzoli, *Cinematography*
Gianni di Venanzo, *Editor* Ruggero Mastroianni,
Music Nino Rota, colour, 145 minutes.
Cast: Giulietta Masina (Giulietta Boldrini), Mario
Pisu (Giorgio), Sandra Milo (Susy/Iris/Fanny), Lou
Gilbert (grandfather), Caterina Boratto (Giulietta's
mother), Luisa Della Noce (Adele), Sylva Koscina
(Sylva), Valentina Cortese (Val).
Juliet of the Spirits is a nightmare exploring the fears
and fantasies of a bourgeois housewife.

Toby Dammit *(1968)*

Episode in the compilation film *Tre passi nel delirio*
(*Spirits of the Dead, Histoires Extraordinaires*, 1968)
Crew: *Director* Federico Fellini, *Writers* Federico
Fellini & Bernardino Zapponi, *Producers* Alberto
Grimaldi & Raymond Eger, *Cinematography*
Giuseppe Rotunno, *Editor* Ruggero Mastroianni,
Music Nino Rota, colour, 37 minutes.
Cast: Terence Stamp (Toby Dammit), Salvo Randone
(Father Spagna), Antonia Pietrosi (actress), Polidor
(old actor), Marina Yaru (the devil as a little girl with
ball).
Toby Dammit is a gloomy episode about a beleaguered actor haunted by sinister visions.

De Santis, *Editor* Ruggero Mastroianni, *Music* Nino Rota, colour, 60 minutes.
Cast (as themselves): Federico Fellini, Giulietta Masina, Marcello Mastroianni, Marina Boratto, Caterina Boratto.
Fellini: A Director's Notebook is an introspective documentary about Fellini's films.

I clowns *(The Clowns, 1970)*

Crew: *Director* Federico Fellini, *Writers* Federico Fellini & Bernardino Zapponi, *Producers* Ugo Guerra & Elio Scardamaglia, *Cinematography* Dario di Palma, *Editor* Ruggero Mastroianni, *Music* Nino Rota, colour, 92 minutes.
Cast (as themselves): Federico Fellini, Liana Orfei, Tristan Rémy, Anita Ekberg, Victoria Chaplin, Baptiste, Père Loriot, Riccardo Billi, Fanfulla.
The Clowns is a patchwork ode to the circus and its tragi-comic performers.

Fellini-Satyricon *(Fellini's Satyricon, 1969)*

Crew: *Director* Federico Fellini, *Writers* Federico Fellini & Bernardino Zapponi (based on *Satyricon* by Titus Petronius), *Producer* Alberto Grimaldi, *Cinematography* Giuseppe Rotunno, *Editor* Ruggero Mastroianni, *Music* Nino Rota, colour, 138 minutes.
Cast: Martin Potter (Encolpio), Hiram Keller (Ascilto), Max Born (Gitone), Mario Romagnoli (Trimalchione), Fanfulla (Vernacchio), Gordon Mitchell (robber), Alain Cuny (Lica), Donyale Luna (Enotea), Danika La Loggia (Scintilla).
Fellini's Satyricon is a costly, colourful historical epic about amorality and excess.

Block-notes di un regista
(Fellini: A Director's Notebook, 1969)

Crew: *Director & writer* Federico Fellini, *Producer* Peter Goldfarb, *Cinematography* Pasquale

Roma *(Fellini's Roma, 1972)*

Crew: *Director* Federico Fellini, *Writers* Federico Fellini & Bernardino Zapponi, *Producer* Turi Vasile, *Cinematography* Giuseppe Rotunno, *Editor* Ruggero Mastroianni, *Music* Nino Rota, colour, 128 minutes.
Cast: Peter Gonzales (young Fellini), Fiona Florence (Dolores), Pia De Doses (princess), Alvaro Vitali (dancer), Federico Fellini, Marcello Mastroianni, Gore Vidal, Anna Magnani, Alberto Sordi (as themselves).
Roma is a fantastical, autobiographical study of the Italian capital city.

Amarcord *(I Remember, 1973)*

Crew: *Director* Federico Fellini, *Writers* Federico Fellini & Tonino Guerra, *Producer* Franco Cristaldi, *Cinematography* Giuseppe Rotunno,

Editor Ruggero Mastroianni, *Music* Nino Rota, colour, 123 minutes.
Cast: Bruno Zanin (Titta), Pupella Maggio (Miranda), Armando Brancia (Aurelio), Nando Orfei (Lallo), Peppino Ianigro (Titta's grandfather), Ciccio Ingrassia (Uncle Teo), Magali Noël (Gradisca), Josiane Tanzilli (Volpina).
Amarcord is an impressionistic and heartfelt ode to growing pains, set in a seaside town.

Il Casanova di Federico Fellini
(Fellini's Casanova, 1976)

Crew: *Director* Federico Fellini, *Writers* Federico Fellini & Bernardino Zapponi, Andrea Zanzotto and Tonino Guerra (lyrics), *Producer* Alberto Grimaldi, *Cinematography* Giuseppe Rotunno, *Editor* Ruggero Mastroianni, *Music* Nino Rota, colour, 163 minutes.

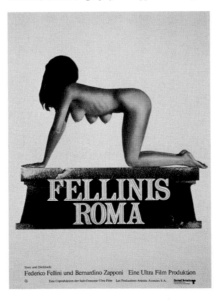

Cast: Donald Sutherland (Casanova), Cicely Browne (Madame d'Urfé), Tina Aumont (Henriette), Margareth Clementi (Maddalena), Olimpia Carlisi (Isabella), Daniel Emilfork (Dubois), Sandy Allen (the giantess), Claretta Algrandi (Marcolina).
Fellini's Casanova is an expensive saga about the life of one of Italy's most famous historical figures.

Prova d'orchestra
(Orchestra Rehearsal, 1979)
Crew: *Director* Federico Fellini, *Writers* Federico Fellini & Brunello Rondi, *Producers* Daimo Cinematografica and RAI, Albatros Produktion, *Cinematography* Giuseppe Rotunno, *Editor* Ruggero Mastroianni, *Music* Nino Rota, colour, 72 minutes.
Cast: Baldwin Baas (orchestra conductor), David Mauhsell (first violinist), Francesco Aluigi (second violinist), Elisabeth Labi (pianist), Ronaldo Bonacchi (contrabassoon), Giovanni Javarone (tuba), Andy Miller (oboe).

Orchestra Rehearsal is a political allegory in which an angry band of musicians revolt against their dictatorial conductor.

La città delle donne *(City of Women, 1980)*
Crew: *Director* Federico Fellini, *Writers* Federico Fellini, Bernardino Zapponi & Brunello Rondi, *Producers* Opera Film Produzione and Gaumont, *Cinematography* Giuseppe Rotunno, *Editor* Ruggero Mastroianni, *Music* Luis Bacalov, colour, 140 minutes.
Cast: Marcello Mastroianni (Snàporaz), Anna Prucnal (Snàporaz's wife), Bernice Stegers (mysterious woman on train), Ettore Manni (Katzone), Donatella Damiani and Rosaria Tafuri (soubrettes).
City of Women is a fantasy about a philanderer who receives a rude awakening at a feminist convention.

E la nave va *(And the Ship Sails On, 1983)*
Crew: *Director* Federico Fellini, *Writers* Federico Fellini & Tonino Guerra, Andrea Zanzotto (opera lyrics), *Producer* Franco Cristaldi, *Cinematography* Giuseppe Rotunno, *Editor* Ruggero Mastroianni, *Music* Gianfranco Plenizio, colour, 132 minutes.
Cast: Freddie Jones (Orlando), Barbara Jefford (Ildebranda Cuffari), Janet Suzman (Edmea Tetua), Vittorio Poletti (Aureliano Fuciletto), Peter Cellier (Sir Reginald Dongby), Norma West (Lady Violet Dongby), Pina Bausch (Princess).
And the Ship Sails On is a nostalgic drama set at sea, following the intrigues onboard a boat carrying the ashes of an opera singer.

Ginger e Fred *(Ginger and Fred, 1985)*
Crew: *Director* Federico Fellini, *Writers* Federico Fellini, Tullio Pinelli & Tonino Guerra, *Producer* Alberti Grimaldi, *Cinematography* Tonino Delli Colli, *Editors* Nino Baragli, Ugo De Rossi & Ruggero Mastroianni, *Music* Nicola Piovani, colour, 127 minutes.
Cast: Giulietta Masina (Ginger), Marcello Mas-

troianni (Fred), Franco Fabrizi (master of ceremonies of variety show), Frederick Ledenburg (admiral), Augusto Poderosi (transvestite), Jacques Henri Lartigue (priest).
Ginger and Fred is a sentimental drama in which a couple of old-time dancers are reunited on a television show.

Intervista *(Interview, 1987)*
Crew: *Director* Federico Fellini, *Writers* Federico Fellini & Gianfranco Angelucci, *Producer* Ibrahim Moussa, *Cinematography* Tonino Delli Colli, *Editor* Nino Baragli, *Music* Nicola Piovani, colour, 113 minutes.
Cast: Sergio Rubini (journalist), Paola Liguori (film star), Maurizio Mein (assistant director), Nadia Ottaviani (custodian of Cinecittà's archives), Anita Ekberg, Federico Fellini, Marcello Mastroianni (as themselves).
Intervista is a pseudo-documentary set around Rome's Cinecittà studios.

La voce della luna
(The Voice of the Moon, 1990)
Crew: *Director* Federico Fellini, *Writers* Federico Fellini, Tullio Pinelli & Ermanno Cavazzoni, *Producers* Mario and Vittorio Cecchi, *Cinematography* Tonino Delli Colli, *Editor* Nino Baragli, *Music* Nicola Piovani, colour, 118 minutes.
Cast: Roberto Benigni (Ivo Salvini), Paolo Villaggio (Prefect Gonnella), Marisa Tomasi (Marisa), Nadia Ottaviani (Aldina Ferruzzi), Algelo Orlando (Nestore), Uta Schmidt (Ivo's grandmother), George Taylor (Marisa's lover).
The Voice of the Moon is a portrait of the modern and the mad.

Bibliography

Biographies
- Alpert, Hollis: *Fellini: A Life*. New York 1986
- Baxter, John: *Fellini*. New York 1994
- Kezich, Tullio: *Fellini*. New York 1993

Books by Fellini
- Fellini, Federico: *Fare un film*. Turin 1980
- Fellini, Federico: *Fellini on Fellini*. New York 1996
- Fellini, Federico: *Un regista a Cinecittà*. Milan 1988

Memoirs
- Chandler, Charlotte: *I, Fellini*. New York 2001
- Costantini, Costanzo (ed.): *Conversations with Fellini*. San Diego/New York 1995
- Grazzini, Giovanni: *Federico Fellini: Comments on Film*. Fresno 1988

Books about Fellini
- Agel, Geneviève: *Les chemins de Fellini*. Paris 1956
- Betti, Liliana: *Fellini*. Boston 1979
- Budgen, Suzanne: *Fellini*. London 1966
- Bondanella, Peter: *The Cinema of Federico Fellini*. Princeton 1992
- Bondanella, Peter: *The Films of Federico Fellini*. Cambridge 2002
- Boyer, Deena: *The Two Hundred Days of 8 1/2*. New York 1964
- Burke, Frank: *Federico Fellini: Variety Lights to La Dolce Vita*. Boston 1984
- Collet, Jean: *La création selon Fellini*. Paris 1990
- Costello, Donald: *Fellini's Road*. Notre Dame 1983
- De Santi, Pier Marco: *I disegni di Fellini*. Rome 1982
- Fantuzzi, Virgilio: *Il vero Fellini*. Rome 1994
- Fava, Claudio G. and Viganò, Aldo: *The Films of Federico Fellini*. Secaucus 1984
- Giacci, Vittorio (ed.): *La voce della luce: Federico Fellini*. Rome 1995
- Grau, Jordi: *Fellini desde Barcelona*. Barcelona 1985
- Hughes, Eileen: *On the Set of Fellini Satyricon*. New York 1971
- Kezich, Tullio: *Fellini del giorno dopo con un alfabetiere felliniano*. Rimini 1996
- Kezich, Tullio: *Il dolce cinema*. Milan 1978
- Milo, Sandra: *Caro Federico*. Milan 1982
- Murray, Edward: *Fellini the Artist*. New York 1985
- Nemiz, Andrea: *Vita, dolce vita*. Rome 1983
- Rondi, Brunello: *Il cinema di Fellini*. Rome 1965
- Rosenthal, Stuart: *The Cinema of Federico Fellini*. South Brunswick 1976
- Salachas, Gilbert: *Federico Fellini: An Investigation Into His Films and Philosophy*. New York 1969
- Solmi, Angelo: *Fellini*. New York 1977
- Strich, Christian (ed.): *Fellini's Films*. New York 1977
- Tornabuoni, Lietta: *Federico Fellini*. New York 1995
- Zanelli, Dario: *Nel mondo di Federico*. Turin 1987

Documentaries
- Ciao Federico! (1970)
- Fellini: The Director as Creator (1970)
- Real Dreams (1987)
- Wizards, Clowns and Honest Liars (1978)
- Fellini: I'm a Big Liar (2001)

Websites
- www.federicofellini.it – Federico Fellini Foundation
- www.cinecitta.com – Cinecittà Official Site

Notes

1. Fellini, Federico: *Fellini on Fellini*. New York 1996. Pg 51.
2. 'The Pilgrim (Chapter 33)' Written by Kris Kristofferson. Resaca Music Publishing Co. From *Cisco Pike*, CBS 1971.
3. Chandler, Charlotte: *I, Fellini*. New York 2001. Pg 7.
4. Chandler, Charlotte: *I, Fellini*. New York 2001. Pg 71.
5. Samuels, Charles Thomas: *Encountering Directors*. New York 1972. Pg 118.
6. Costantini, Costanzo (ed.): *Conversations with Fellini*. San Diego/New York 1995. Pg 33.
7. Fellini, Federico: *Fellini on Fellini*. New York 1996. Pg 73.
8. Baxter, John: *Fellini*. New York 1994. Pg 69.
9. Grazzini, Giovanni: *Federico Fellini: Comments on Film*. Fresno 1988. Pg 132.
10. Douchet, Jean. Article in *Cahiers du cinéma*. Issue 132. Paris June 1962.
11. Grazzini, Giovanni: *Federico Fellini: Comments on Film*. Fresno 1988. Pg 158.
12. Grazzini, Giovanni: *Federico Fellini: Comments on Film*. Fresno 1988. Pg 162.
13. Kael, Pauline: *For Keeps*. New York 1994. Pgs 70–71.
14. Bory, Jean-Louis. Article in *Le nouvel observateur*. Paris 15 December 1969.
15. Dorigo, Francesco. Article in *Il Piccolo*. Trieste 31 August 1970.
16. Baxter, John: *Fellini*. New York 1994. Pg 261.
17. Costantini, Costanzo (ed.): *Conversations with Fellini*. San Diego/New York 1995. Pg 91.
18. Canby, Vincent. Article in *The New York Times*. New York 12 February 1977.
19. Grazzini, Giovanni: *Federico Fellini: Comments on Film*. Fresno 1988. Pg 219.
20. Costantini, Costanzo (ed.): *Conversations with Fellini*. San Diego/New York 1995.
21. Fellini, Federico: *Fellini on Fellini*. New York 1996.
22. Grazzini, Giovanni: *Federico Fellini: Comments on Film*. Fresno 1988.
23. Baxter, John: *Fellini*. New York 1994.
24. Chandler, Charlotte: *I, Fellini*. New York 2001.

Federico Fellini and Giulietta Masina in Venice (c. 1955)